A JOHN CATT PUBLICATION

G000108227

TAUGHT NOT CAUGHT

EDUCATING FOR 21st CENTURY CHARACTER

NICKY MORGAN

First Published 2017

by John Catt Educational Ltd,
12 Deben Mill Business Centre,
Old Maltings Approach,
Melton, Woodbridge IP12 1BL

Tel: +44 (0) 1394 389850
Fax: +44 (0) 1394 386893
Email: enquiries@johncatt.com
Website: www.johncatt.com

© **2017 Nicky Morgan**
Illustrations © Oliver Caviglioli

All rights reserved.

No part of this publication may be reproduced,
stored in a retrieval system, transmitted in any
form or by any means, electronic, mechanical,
photocopying, recording, or otherwise, without
the prior permission of the publishers.

Opinions expressed in this publication are those
of the contributors and are not necessarily
those of the publishers or the editors. We cannot
accept responsibility for any errors or omissions.

ISBN: 978 1 911382 33 1

Set and designed by
John Catt Educational Limited

Praise for *Taught Not Caught*

"The key point – that a true one nation government needs to equip all its children with knowledge *and* character – is one which is too infrequently recognised by both proponents and opponents of a traditional education, and it is to Nicky's credit that this is made explicit."
Jonathan Simons, Director of Policy and Advocacy, the Varkey Foundation

"An excellent and provocative account of the ways some schools are successfully helping their pupils develop positive personality characteristics, the benefits which come from such things as mental reliance and grit, and ways in which character can be assessed."
Barnaby Lenon, chair, Independent Schools Council

"My hope is that this very readable, carefully crafted book will signal a national renaissance, which will emphasise the urgent need to support children to develop positive character traits in values-based schools."
Dr. Neil Hawkes, founder, Values-based Education, founder of the International Education Trust

"Nicky Morgan was instructive, as Secretary of State for Education, in placing character education at the forefront of UK educational policy. It is gratifying to see that she now continues with her efforts at a more theoretical level by illustrating her own vision of how to educate for 21st-century character."
Professor Kristján Kristjánsson, Jubilee Centre for Character and Virtues, University of Birmingham

"In chapter 4 in particular, the case for embedding social action in a young person's journey is made compellingly. Examples from some of our #iwill champion schools and colleges show the double benefit of building character and virtue, and making a positive difference to the community."
Charlotte Hill, Chief Executive, Step Up to Serve

"Provides some great examples of schools underpinning their academic ambitions for pupils with thoughtful work on character development. Nicky Morgan shows how paying attention to this aspect of education supports improved outcomes for all pupils."
Mary Myatt, adviser, speaker and author

"As Nicky Morgan makes clear, the current evidence on how to build these skills is limited, and rightly presses us all to do more and focus efforts on building high quality research to help schools."
Kevan Collins, chief executive, Education Endowment Foundation

"Nicky Morgan's advocacy of character education while she was Secretary of State for Education was a breath of sanity in an otherwise instrumental period of English education. This book shows that she was and is serious about embedding character in all schools to create as a contribution to one-nation thinking on this important topic."
Professor Bill Lucas, Director, Centre for Real-World Learning at the University of Winchester

"An authoritative guide to character education that illuminates both why we need it and how we can do it even better than we do now. Insightful, brimming with inspiring examples, and winningly personal."
Angela Duckworth, Founder and CEO, Character Lab

"Nicky Morgan's powerful and deeply felt case for the re-establishment of Character Education at the heart of schools is the clarion call that must be heard."
Sir Anthony Seldon

Contents

Of course, when pressure to get academic results is combined with a tight funding environment, schools can find it hard to make time to recalibrate their offer. Yet with the many examples that Nicky provides in this book, she convincingly shows that good character education is something that helps schools succeed, not something that schools can find time for only once they are successful.

Foreword

Politicians are fond of describing decisions they make as 'brave' or 'difficult', but it is rare to find one whose actions can genuinely be described in those terms. However, as someone who was watching closely at the time, I think it is a fair description of Nicky Morgan's decision, as Secretary of State, to place character development at the heart of the government's approach to education.

The reason it was an act of political courage is that prioritising character education went against the two prevailing arguments in England's education debate. On one side, there are the relativists who think that character is purely subjective, if not downright oppressive, and that schools should have no business getting involved in such dubious ethical activities. On the other side are what are called the neo-trads, those who – rightly, in my view – believe that every child can and should benefit from a broad, knowledge-rich academic education but who too often believe that any deviation from that purist view is a kind of heresy, a Trojan Horse for the relativism they fight against.

In her straightforward and no nonsense style, Nicky cut through this and asserted that education should be about 'academics plus character' with a three part appeal to tradition, evidence and common sense. And it is that argument which she brings to life so compellingly in this excellent book.

For most of human civilization, the idea that educating young people should *not* be about developing both their minds and their moral sense would have seemed bizarre. In this famous speech on the purpose of education, Martin Luther King said "… intelligence is not enough. Intelligence plus character – that is the goal of true education", and in making that point he was appealing to the great education traditions of both West and East, Aristotle as well as Confucius. It is only in the last 100 years that we have become confused about the purpose of education, and swung around from extreme to extreme.

The appeal to wisdom is dramatically strengthened by the evidential base, which is clearly and concisely set out in the book. Character is a meaningful concept, it can be taught and learned, and having or acquiring positive character traits is associated with a range of positive life outcomes, from mental wellbeing to employment to longer life. These facts are becoming better understood from a range of research programmes, some of which were set up by money provided by an innovative grant scheme that Nicky herself set up.

Finally, there is the appeal to common sense. Politicians are sometimes accused of being out of touch, but in reality they meet many more and a wider variety of ordinary people than most people ever do, and have a keen sense of their preferences. And virtually every parent wants their child to, in the words of the US-based KIPP school chain, "work hard and be nice". This is confirmed by polling from the Jubilee Centre of Character and Virtues, who found that nearly nine-in-ten parents want their child's education to focus on both academic learning and character development.

In making the argument in favour of character, and in setting up a number of incisive programmes and policy changes aimed at promoting character education, Nicky lit the blue touch paper. In the interests of disclosure, I should mention that Floreat Education – the academy trust I founded and which is generously described in the book – was a recipient of one of the character awards Nicky instigated. With the funding, we developed a character curriculum for infant-aged pupils. Not only has this curriculum provided popular and effective in our own three schools, it has garnered interest both nationally and internationally.

What this experience, and being involved in the character education movement more generally, has shown me is that teachers are crying out for good quality resources and leadership so that they can re-engage in the classical idea of developing and moulding young people's characters for the good.

What has been lacking are curriculum models, pedagogical approaches, a language of character, and 'permission' from the powers that be to make character education a priority. There are some diehards who do not think that is a teacher's role, but most teachers are – unsurprisingly – deeply committed to seeing their pupils turn out well, equipped to live happy and successful lives.

That is not to say that, despite Nicky's ongoing efforts, character education has been thoroughly (re)established at the heart of education. A number of arguments still rage and are explored in this book, such whether character development can be quantified, the extent to which character is genetically determined, or whether character education amounts to anything more than the old public school mentality of 'good manners plus sport'. And, of course, when pressure to get academic results is combined with a tight funding environment, schools can find it hard to make time to recalibrate their offer. Yet with the many examples that Nicky provides in this book, she convincingly shows that good character education is something that *helps* schools succeed, not something that schools can find time for only once they are successful.

The final word should go to the future. I'm unconvinced that education needs to be radically reimagined to take account of jobs of the future. After all, it's pretty unlikely that a future economy dominated by AI and robotics is going to need people who are less knowledgable than they are today.

But consider the taxi driver of the 2030s. Her car will drive itself, although she will still need some sophisticated technical skills in case of technological failure. However, her eyes will not be on the road, they will be on her passengers and her primary role will be to ensure that they have an enjoyable and interesting journey. She may be trained to look for signs of mental or physical illness or distress, and to be able to signpost help.

If that is the job of the future – people facing, compassionate, service-oriented, resilient, agile, broad in scope, not so much a cog in a machine but a temporary guide through the complexities of life - then character will be the *sine qua non* of a good education. And because of Nicky's leadership, first as Education Secretary and now through this book, we are getting closer to ensuring all young people get the academics plus character education they need to flourish.

Lord James O'Shaughnessy, August 2017

Author's note

As I write in the Introduction, I've been fortunate enough to hold one of the best jobs in the UK Cabinet – Secretary of State for Education. This gave me the platform to encourage the Department for Education, its excellent and committed civil servants (particularly, in the case of the character work, Juliet Chua) and schools across the country, to focus on how we develop the character of the next generation.

I remain immensely grateful to my Special Advisers who worked so hard for me and to deliver the 2014/15 and 2015/16 Government's education agenda – Luke Tryl, Chris Wilkins, Lee Davis and George Looker – and to my Private Office: you all know who you are.

During my time as Secretary of State I was lucky enough to meet and to be inspired by some very talented people in this field. I'd like to thank Professor James Arthur, Sir Anthony Seldon, Neil and Jane Hawkes, James O'Shaughnessy and Sir Gus O'Donnell for their encouragement, particularly when I told them I was going to write this book.

I'd like to thank Corey Dixon and Jessica Davies and the team at Parthenon EY for their invaluable research support, and to also thank Jonah Surkes, Chris Paterson, Ali Hussain, Tony and Angie Russell, Fiona Pender, Rod Bristow, Christine Hodgson, Nick Wergan, Peter Blackwell, Kevan Collins, Steve Harris and Richard Gould for pointing me in the right direction and sharing their expertise.

Additionally, I thank David Willetts and Michael Hayman for their personal encouragement and Alex Sharratt at John Catt Educational for his support when my manuscript was delayed by an unexpected election!

This book just wouldn't have been possible though without the generous support of the schools I visited and the Heads whose brains I picked. Being a Headteacher is a big job and yet all of the Heads and teams I visited were very generous in giving me their time and views – in particular James Malley, Jo Dibb, Gary Lewis (King's Langley) & Ruth Jennings, Gary Lewis (Gordano), Denise Newsome & Sara Fletcher, David Dennis, Sally Sixsmith & Lindsay Mason and Shane Ierston & Andrew Reay. Thank you to them too for entering the DfE's Character Awards in the first place.

Final thanks are due to Jonathan and Alex for putting up with me and to my parents who made such a big thing about character in the first place.

Needless to say any and all errors are mine.

Nicky Morgan, August 2017

People often ask what we mean when we talk about character. For me character traits are those qualities that enhance us as people: persistence, the ability to work with others, to show humility in the joy of success and resilience in the face of failure.

Character is about being self-aware, playing an active role within communities. It's about selflessness and self-discipline as well as playing a full role in society.

It's fair to say that's a long list of traits! But that goes to the very heart of this debate — there is no one clear definition of character.

There is no one easy list of boxes to tick. We don't want to set down rigid guidelines on this because character isn't a one-size-fits-all concept.

It isn't just one thing. It's a combination of the traits that set people apart so they can achieve their dreams.

SPEECH, JANUARY 2016

INTRODUCTION

Introduction

The English education system is only doing half the job it needs to do to prepare our children for the 21st century. In a world where many of the jobs of tomorrow haven't even been invented, where technology is changing our world increasingly rapidly and where people are likely to dip in and out of self-employment, employers are putting an ever greater premium on character traits such as resilience, persistence, grit, leadership, self-awareness and self-efficacy.

But this isn't just about our working lives. History is littered with examples of people who have bounced back from failure – generals, monarchs, inventors, novelists. What about the stories of those who didn't bounce back? Who else might we have included in history books if they had one of the key character traits: the ability to cope with setbacks, to learn from their mistakes and take control of the situations they found themselves in – labelled as "stickability" in one school I visited.

These traits and the values underpinning them stand all of us in great stead for an ever more complicated life and, because schools shape our society, the more people we have with well-formed characters the stronger and more values-driven our society will be.

At what point did the English schools system stop cultivating these traits, adopt an attitude of moral ambivalence and say that teaching was solely about an "academic transaction" as described by Professor A H Halsey? As the Jubilee Centre's 2017 Framework for Character Education in

Schools puts it, "[Schools] should help prepare for the tests of life, rather than simply a life of tests."

What is character? How do people develop their character? What do they have to do or experience to build those traits? Can these traits be taught? I firmly believe the answer is yes and this book shows why, how and what is already happening across England, because there are schools which are not waiting to be told to prioritise character education.

Why is it the case that only some of our schools, often in the independent sector, focus on the development of strong character traits, whilst also managing to combine this with an excellent academic and rigorous education? A truly one-nation government must not accept that only some people deserve the opportunities to build character that will help them to get on in life.

If we don't provide all children with those opportunities to build character (often supported through extracurricular activities) then they will be at a disadvantage no matter how many SATs and GCSEs they pass. That is not only unfair to them but also detrimental to the future success of our country. How do we stand a chance of healing the divisions in our country if our education system isn't preparing the next generation to deal with the challenges of the world we live in rather than be threatened or left behind by them?

I've had the privilege of holding one of the best jobs in the UK cabinet. As Education Secretary I visited many schools and could see those schools where the Headteacher and all the staff were building not just knowledgeable young people but also engaged and confident pupils. Where they were helping them to develop values which would set them up for life, to be aware of their community, to identify their passions in life and to help them to flourish.

And I could see those schools which professed to do these things but didn't, those which told me they simply didn't have the time due to the demands of the curriculum and their governors or parents and those who told me they didn't need to bother with all this "soft skills stuff" and that an academic curriculum was their only goal.

A rich education full of character development is not an alternative to an academic knowledge-rich education. They are two sides of the same coin and both are necessary to prepare our young people for success and stability in the 21st century.

The meaning of the Latin word 'education' is to "lead and draw out that which lies within". As Chris Wright, the Director of Education at Woodard Schools, and Bill Watkin, the Director of SSAT, say in their book *Schools for Human Flourishing*, "Education is about more than the flight towards academic success and employment. It is, at its heart, about human flourishing."

As Tom Harrison, Ian Morris and John Ryan state in their book *Teaching Character in the Primary Classroom*, "If true and full education is about preparing young people for their futures, then the development of character virtues is a central part of this preparation. Society demands humans who are, amongst other things compassionate, courageous, resilient, honest and respectful."

In a speech in January 2016 I said:

People often ask what we mean when we talk about character. For me, character traits are those qualities that enhance us as people: persistence, the ability to work with others, to show humility in the joy of success and resilience in the face of failure.

Character is about being self-aware, playing an active role within communities. It's about selflessness and self-discipline as well as playing a full role in society. It's fair to say that's a long list of traits!

But that goes to the very heart of this debate – there is no one clear definition of character. There is no one easy list of boxes to tick.

We don't want to set down rigid guidelines on this because character isn't a one-size-fits-all concept. It isn't just one thing. It's a combination of the traits that set people apart so they can achieve their dreams.

If schools shape society then the person who shapes a school and is key to making sure children within them flourish is the Headteacher. Without their leadership, support and drive, attempts to build characterful children will fail. But they also need the support and buy-in of their staff and families. This book therefore also looks at the influence of adult role models – deliberate and accidental.

Building characterful children is also a way of increasing mental wellbeing and resilience. That isn't to say that a focus on character will stop some young people developing mental ill health. There will always be those who need professional support to help them to overcome such mental health challenges.

But I do believe that growing up today is more complicated than it has ever been. Rapid technological change, longer and more demanding working lives for parents and grandparents, the daily deluge of information, the competitiveness and relentlessness of 21st century life make mental resilience even more important. Character education, with its emphasis on self-belief, self-reflection and self-confidence, prepares today's students for current and future challenges and gives them the ability to take control of any situation they find themselves in.

This book also looks at whether building characterful children has a positive impact on academic attainment and asks if character should be assessed or whether that would provide the wrong incentive. The importance of extracurricular activities is also examined – including the fact that the availability and take-up of those activities is, in itself, a victim of social injustice. And what are employers saying about the need for the non-cognitive skills which character education develops?

In writing this book I've had the privilege of visiting some of the schools who won Department for Education character awards. Hearing their stories, looking at the work they've done to promote character education and identify the values they want to embed in their schools and seeing how positive they are about this area of their school life has confirmed to me that focusing on character sits alongside gaining knowledge. In fact, the former helps the latter. The generosity of the schools enables me to capture key examples and bring character education to life.

I am very grateful to everyone I met for their generosity and enthusiasm. Stepping back into school visits, having been Secretary of State, was nerve-wracking but everyone I met in the course of writing this book was extremely welcoming.

Change in education doesn't happen by accident. It needs a deliberate push. Public awareness needs to be raised, government needs to make it clear to those in the education system that this is a priority and they will support it and, most importantly, the frontline – namely schools, Heads, teachers, governors and communities – need to be enabled to create the conditions to allow systemic change to happen, to take hold and to grow.

Education is the greatest investment we can make in the future of our country. And the greatest investment the education system can make in our pupils is to ensure they gain both knowledge and character.

CHAPTER 1

WHAT DOES 'CHARACTER' MEAN — VALUES, VIRTUES AND TRAITS AND WHY DOES HAVING IT MATTER?

❝ CHOICE

This book argues that helping students (and those around them) to develop the skills to choose between vice and virtue should not be left to chance but should be deliberately and explicitly taught.

❝ BEYOND SCHOOLS

Of course, the ways to help young people to develop character traits which enable them to flourish is not confined just to schools or activities within school hours.

❝ LANGUAGE

...students picked up the character language and used terms such as self-control and staying power without hesitation.

❝ EVIDENCE

The evidence shows there is no clear answer but a 2016 University of Edinburgh study would suggest that lifelong stability of personality is relatively low, meaning that personality is not fixed.

❝ MALLEABLE SKILLS

In terms of which skills are malleable the review states that self-efficacy, motivation, meta-cognitive strategies (ie the methods used to help students understand the way they learn), social skills and coping strategies can be fostered in some contexts and with some age groups...

❝ PERSONALITY TRAITS

However grit, creativity and self-control are more akin to personality traits and therefore relatively fixed.

> *Character is, in the long run, the decisive factor in the life of individuals and of nations alike* – Theodore Roosevelt
>
> *It is not by muscle, speed, or physical dexterity that great things are achieved, but by reflection, force of character, and judgement* – Marcus Tullius Cicero
>
> *Character is the glue of the school* – Carl Ward, Headteacher, Haywood Academy, February 2017

What is the definition of character and how is it different from values? We tried hard in the Department for Education not to define what we meant by 'character education'. Why? Because we would then have spent a long time explaining and justifying our definition rather than working on how good character education can take root and flourish.

There are many, many quotations from myriad famous, not so famous and infamous people about 'character'. I've chosen two historic quotes and one contemporary one for the start of this chapter.

Dictionaries define 'character' as "the distinguishing qualities of a person; a person's moral qualities, moral strength".

Dr Neil Hawkes, the founder of the Values-based Education Trust, prefers to focus on values which make up a person's character. He defines a value as "a principle that guides our thinking and behaviour" and says that "values help to determine the formation of our character".

The Jubilee Centre for Character and Virtues at Birmingham University, meanwhile, instead focus on virtues. They identify four types of "virtues" – civic, moral, performance and intellectual.

These can be further broken down as follows:

- Civic: service and volunteering; neighbourliness; citizenship; community awareness and spirit; social justice
- Moral: courage; compassion; gratitude; honesty and integrity; justice; humility or modesty; self-discipline; tolerance; respect
- Performance: resilience; perseverance, grit and determination; leadership; teamwork; motivation or ambition; confidence
- Intellectual: reflection; focus; critical thinking; reason and judgement; curiosity; communication; resourcefulness; open-mindedness

The work of the Jubilee Centre on modern virtues is strongly influenced by the work of Aristotle who wrote about his theories over 2000 years ago. Aristotle wrote extensively on philosophy, science, literature and politics and he set up his own college, the Lyceum, in Athens in 336 BC. He believed that humans possessed a natural moral end – a good flourishing life, a state of being an excellent human – and to achieve this end was good in itself.

Virtues were those character traits that were conducive to achieving this end or a part of it. Virtues such as nobility, courage, temperance and fortitude were good virtues to have and those to avoid included injustice, intemperance and deceitfulness. Aristotle's goal in his work was to describe which qualities constituted an excellent character.

In *Teaching Character in the Primary Classroom*, Tom Harrison, Ian Morris and John Ryan identify a meta-virtue which is important to an Aristotelian understanding of character – phronesis, meaning practical wisdom. They state, "practical wisdom helps pupils to put the other virtues into practice – as such it should be considered a moderating or enabling virtue. In some cases it might be required to help pupils choose between vice and virtue."

21

This book argues that helping students (and those around them) to develop the skills to choose between vice and virtue should not be left to chance but should be deliberately and explicitly taught. Learning about virtue is not the same as learning to be virtuous. Having "virtue knowledge" is different from being "virtue literate". These differences, many argue, need to be explicitly taught.

As Harrison, Morris and Ryan write, "Schools of Character might be described like a stick of rock – cut through them anywhere and you will find character education going on either implicitly or explicitly."

Perhaps the best illustration of character education and the acquisition of "practical wisdom" is to consider what many schools are already doing. The new University of Birmingham School, which I had the pleasure of opening in 2015, is supported by the Jubilee Centre. The school website says, "Character Education is about acquiring and strengthening virtue – traits that sustain a well-rounded life and a thriving society; values such as compassion, humility, sensitivity, creativity, curiosity, determination and resilience."

The school has developed a brand new curriculum and resources for timetabled lessons to support the development of character. This focus also runs through their form periods, college system, meal times and all enrichment activities.

Chapter 9 sets out how a school can identify the traits it particularly wants to prioritise for discussion and development. Being clear about the traits and getting support from all members of a school community are critical to ensuring character education success.

Schools such as the excellent Goldbeaters Primary in Barnet, which I visited, have a full statement of their vision and values on their website. They make it clear that, by the time their pupils reach Year 6, they will have developed a list of positive traits which make them a "Golden Child" as follows:

Golden Child

We would describe a Golden Child as:

A person who tries their best
A great learner
Responsible, a good decision maker and know right from wrong
A good friend
Kind
Polite and well mannered
Confident about themselves
Positive in attitude
Honest
A good communicator
Respectful and understanding of others
Cool
Resilient
Ambitious
Safe
Strong in commitment
Hard working

By Year 6

A child will be all of the above and also:

a. know his/her academic strengths
b. know his/her talents

My visit to Goldbeaters Primary coincided with a session led by former leading rugby players who were teaching the pupils not so much the rules of the game but the associated traits such as resilience, grit, discipline, aspiration, sportsmanship and teamwork.

Floreat Education was established in 2014 in order to create a family of world-class schools where every child can flourish. As their website says:

We believe strong values are essential to flourishing.

All Floreat schools will foster a core and balanced set of four virtues:

- Curiosity – an intellectual virtue, that refers to open-mindedness, a desire to inquire, and a quest to improve and find out more.
- Honesty – a moral virtue, that calls on us to seek truth both in the world and within our own lives; this also calls for vulnerability and openness to feedback, whatever our status.
- Perseverance – a performance virtue that enables us to keep striving in the face of adversity in pursuit of long-term goals.
- Service – a civic virtue, meaning a commitment to help other people.

Of course, helping young people to develop character traits which enable them to flourish is not confined just to schools or activities within school hours. We will examine this more in Chapter 8 but one example to consider now is ReachOut, a London- and Manchester-based charity that gives disadvantaged young people the individual support they need to achieve their potential and go on to lead good and happy lives. They partner with schools where more than 50% of the students are eligible for free school meals.

The young people are aged 9-18 and have been referred because of low academic attainment, low confidence, low self-esteem, poor behaviour, fragmented home life or because their teachers believe they would benefit from the support of a role model. Ninety per cent of the students are Black, Asian or Minority Ethnic. The four character strengths ReachOut seeks to develop are fairness, self-control, good judgement and staying power. The latter is defined as "resilience, grit, the ability to stick at something, to honour commitments, to see tasks through to the end".

In summer 2017 I visited a ReachOut session at a school in East London with a hugely diverse intake of pupils. What was striking about the session – which was divided into three distinct parts involving supported academic study, a fun team activity and then sport – was how those leading the session talked about character traits all the time. Because of this the students picked up the character language and used terms such as self-control and staying power without hesitation.

The academic study session involved pupils being supported by coaches (many of whom tended to be teachers from other schools giving up their time voluntarily) to help them to be confident about work they were doing at the school.

Talking to one of the ReachOut leaders afterwards she confirmed how important developing character was for the students they are working with. She confessed that she hadn't realised how fundamental these traits were for success until she became aware how many students didn't possess these skills and what a difference she was now seeing in their attainment and confidence as the course continued and these traits were specifically developed.

I think all four strengths that ReachOut seek to develop are hugely important but the last one, staying power, is particularly under-developed in far too many of our young people. It's the reason why good parents consciously or unconsciously keep bugging their children to practise instruments, attend sports practice even when it's wet and windy or keep revising for exams. Without staying power it's almost impossible to succeed because most achievements in life only come through sustained hard work and effort. Just ask our Olympic athletes.

And it's why reality TV shows are so misleading. They make success look too instant and too easy. It would be good to give more exposure to just how long the bands and singers on *The X Factor* have been performing without any public attention before they hit the so-called 'big time'. It's why, when I speak to school audiences, I always emphasise how it took me 21 years to get from signing up to a political party to being elected as an MP.

Resilience is just one trait which character education can focus on. Those currently writing about character tend to focus on a variety of different traits or virtues. The Jubilee Centre, already highlighted above, focuses on character being a set of personal traits, dispositions or 'virtues' that "produce specific moral emotions, inform motivation and guide conduct".

Angela Duckworth, who has written the excellent *Grit*, says that character has a number of different aspects as follows:

Intrapersonal – strengths of Will *eg* Grit, self-control, optimism, growth mindset

Interpersonal – strengths of Heart *eg* Gratitude, social intelligence, larger purpose

Intellectual – strengths of Mind *eg* Zest, curiosity

David Brooks in *The Road to Character* talks about resumé virtues – the skills you bring to the workplace – and eulogy virtues – the ones that are talked about at a person's funeral. He calls the former Adam I and the latter Adam II. Brooks's argument is that Adam I is the career-oriented, ambitious side of our nature and Adam II wants to embody certain moral qualities and that our culture is now focused on developing Adam I and not Adam II.

He says, "We're not more selfish or venal than people in other times but we've lost the understanding of how character is built. The 'crooked timber' moral tradition – based on the awareness of sin and the confrontation with sin – was an inheritance passed down from generation to generation. It gave people a clear sense of how to cultivate the eulogy virtues, how to develop the Adam II side of their nature. Without it, there is a certain superficiality to modern culture, especially in the moral sphere."

Talking about the life of US General and then US President, Dwight Eisenhower, Brooks also says that, "the essential drama of life is the drama to construct character, which is an engraved set of disciplined habits, a settled disposition to do good. The cultivation of Adam II was seen as a necessary foundation for Adam I to flourish."

In his proposed Humility Code he says, "Character is built in the course of your inner confrontation. Character is a set of dispositions, desires and habits that are slowly engraved during the struggle against your own weakness" and, "The things we call character endure over the long term

– courage, honesty, humility."

Brooks is clear that as a society we should be focusing as much if not more on what the Jubilee Centre calls moral virtues rather than performance or intellectual virtues. This is hard territory for public policy-makers to pronounce on, perhaps easier for individual schools, teachers or governors and should certainly be the norm for families and parents.

> *I think all four strengths that ReachOut seek to develop are hugely important but the last one, staying power, is particularly under-developed in far too many of our young people.*

However, an example of how this focus on morals or ethics is possible for a school is given by John Goodey of St John the Baptist Church of England Primary School in Lewisham in *Schools for Human Flourishing*. He talks of the 22 values the school has and how "we immerse the children in this ethical vocabulary so that they develop a moral compass from which they can make effective decisions in their lives".

He explains that when his pupils experience challenge or have problems with behaviour they are supported to draw on the values and the values make sense of their lives.

The diagram on the following page was given to me by James Malley, the Headteacher at Therfield School in Leatherhead, Surrey, a school which was one of the recipients of a 2015 Department for Education Character Award. It is sometimes used in talks and workshops by Bill Lucas, co author of *Educating Ruby*. At the centre it says "Character is Power", and this is surrounded by a list of many desirable traits a person should try to demonstrate – although we both agreed that "Princely Manhood" may be less in keeping with the demands of the 21st century.

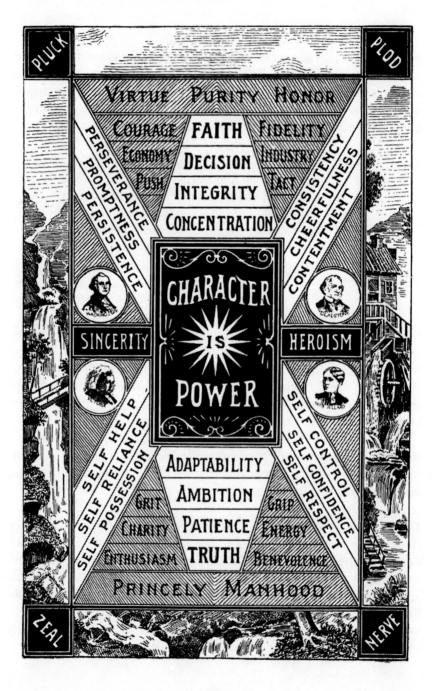

At King's Langley in Hertfordshire, they have identified the three core traits they want to develop in their pupils as:

- Stickability – the ability to stick at something even if it hurts
- Self-regulation – the ability to control your actions and your communications
- Empathy – the ability to put yourself in someone else's shoes

Their work has evolved to include virtues which follow the Jubilee Centre's four key categories of moral, civic, intellectual and performance virtues. Gary Lewis, the Headteacher at King's Langley, has been committed since 2004 to "happy students which has meant developing integrity, moral fortification and resilience". In 2009 the school ethos evolved to identify the three core traits mentioned above. The school also say that they "promote students working towards making the right choices in life – being able to consider the different options and making the right decisions (or, if not the right ones, understanding any consequences)". This has echoes of the definition of character above which is about doing the right thing when no one is watching.

At King's Langley there is a whole-school approach so it is not just students who are expected to develop and demonstrate these traits. The expectation applies to staff, governors and parents too.

Later in the book we will examine how King's Langley and other schools develop the character of their students but it is no secret that everyone is expected to be polite and show good manners and attitudes in school. Both the expected attitudes to learning and subject content have been linked to the traits and virtues. The school has appointed a lead practitioner for character.

At the start of the chapter I used a quote from the Headteacher of Haywood Academy in Burslem near Stoke-on-Trent. When Carl Ward arrived at Haywood one of his first tasks was to re-define the values the school wanted students to exhibit. Carl says, "What is missing from schools not doing well is soul. And character creates soul." He believes that soul comes from the staff at a school so their professional development is very important. This is echoed by the other schools I've visited.

Like other Heads, Carl talks about building social capital and giving his students the belief that they can get results. He also talks about wanting the adults in the school to connect on a personal level with the students to show they really do care what happens to them. In the same way one of the first things Gary Lewis did at King's Langley in Hertfordshire when he arrived there was to incentivise the staff to run extracurricular activities "so the kids were able to achieve".

King's Leadership Academy in Warrington is an inspirational new free school which only opened in 2014 but is already oversubscribed. The school is clear that it places the development of character, service and good citizenship at the heart of everything it does. In its pedagogical practice guide it firmly states:

King's firmly believes in 'character education'. The values and attitudes we live by affect how we relate to other people and our environment; they predispose us to respond in particular ways to people and events, and fashion our outlook on life. By framing our approach to educating our young people within a firm set of values, we hope to help them discover more about themselves and become successful contributing citizens.

The seven pillars of character King's has identified are captured in the abbreviation ASPIRE which stands for:

A – Aspiration and achievement

S – Self-awareness

P – Professionalism

I – Integrity

R – Respect

E – Endeavour

The school has codified the behaviours they want to see students develop on the basis that this will create a positive climate for their learning and eventual success.

The gaining of knowledge, which I believe is at the heart of any successful curriculum and time spent at school, is not secondary to the development of character but intrinsically a reason for developing character.

As defined by these schools the character being developed helps all students to become highly effective and take responsibility for their own education, with the support of the professionals around them who not only impart knowledge and expertise but also model the values and traits the school attaches great importance to.

In their 'Character Counts' booklet King's Leadership states that "a young person's character is the summation of his or her values, attitudes and behaviours. Because those qualities are learned, they can also be purposefully taught. Good character doesn't happen automatically, and it's too important to be left to chance if our mission is to be successful."

This raises the question of whether character can be taught rather than caught. The evidence shows there is no clear answer but a 2016 University of Edinburgh study[1] would suggest that lifelong stability of personality is relatively low, meaning that personality is not fixed. This particular study looked at the interval between the ages of 14 and 77 so the starting point was some way through an individual's school career.

With a big health warning about the unknown impact of external factors, the fact that the tests were self-reported at the age of 77 (at the age of 14 the traits were reported on by teachers) and of course not everyone survived long enough to do all the tests, the study did show stability could only be observed for stability of mood and conscientiousness. Stability did not hold for the other personality characteristics of self-confidence, perseverance, originality or desire to excel.

---

1. www.research.ed.ac.uk/portal/en/publications/personality-stability-from-age-14-to-age-77-years(570f260c-8fa6-4bab-892f-0a0657e573fa).html

The authors conclude that whilst personality changes only gradually throughout life, by old age personality may be quite different from adolescent personality.

An earlier 2013 review by Gutman & Schoon[2] showed that non-cognitive skills are associated with positive outcomes but there is a lack of robust evidence of a causal relationship across many skills and it is also not known how far interventions or teaching can impact on these skills nor what the long-term impacts are.

> *The gaining of knowledge, which I believe is at the heart of any successful curriculum and time spent at school, is not secondary to the development of character but intrinsically a reason for developing character.*

In terms of which skills are malleable the review states that self-efficacy, motivation, meta-cognitive strategies (*ie* the methods used to help students understand the way they learn), social skills and coping strategies can be fostered in some contexts and with some age groups and that these have varying levels of impact on other outcomes such as academic achievement and wellbeing. The review particularly finds that self-efficacy impacts on academic achievement and that meta-cognitive strategies (examined further in Chapter 9) do correlate with academic outcomes. However, grit, creativity and self-control are more akin to personality traits and therefore relatively fixed. The authors found that effective teaching, school environment and social and emotional learning programmes play a role in developing non-cognitive skills.

---

2. The impact of non-cognitive skills on outcomes for young people – Literature review for EEF/ Cabinet Office, November 2013

In the US, James Heckman's multiple reviews of the Perry pre-school project have established the importance of early years education whose lasting impact was not on IQ but on character skills. The impact was lifelong. The conclusion was that early years are the key malleable stage with reinforcement useful during adolescence between the ages of 12 and 15. The character traits influenced were academic motivation (engagement, initiative and persistence) as well as negative externalising behaviour such as lying, cheating, aggression and classroom disruption.

This is supported by a 2004 study for the OECD titled 'Improving Cognitive and Non-Cognitive Skills to Promote Lifetime Success'[3] which found that in early years both cognitive and non-cognitive skills are malleable whilst in adolescents non-cognitive skills are more malleable. The study found that parental involvement is needed to impact on early years interventions whilst adolescents need mentoring. The OECD study concluded that any intervention needs to emulate the mentoring and attachment that successful families give their children.

A 2009 Australian study in primary school settings by Lovat[4] found that the impact of the explicit teaching of values, the modelling of those values and the involvement of families included improvements in academic diligence which was measured by looking at personal endeavour, attentiveness in class, adherence to class rules, observing behaviour amongst children and seeing responsible behaviour in the classroom. The school ambience also improved with schools becoming more self-reflective and qualitative feedback suggesting less fighting and more honesty, although parents noted less of an improvement because they thought the ambience was already positive.

What these studies demonstrate is the correlation between teaching non-cognitive skills and wider outcomes. The potential malleability of certain character traits is clear and therefore there is huge potential for formative institutions, such as schools, as well as families to really influence their

---

3. www.oecd.org/edu/ceri/Fostering-and-Measuring-Skills-Improving-Cognitive-and-Non-Cognitive-Skills-to-Promote-Lifetime-Success.pdf
4. www.curriculum.edu.au/verve/_resources/Project_to_Test_and_Measure_the_Impact_of_Values_Education.pdf

development as demonstrated by the schools mentioned in this book and the many others making character education a priority.

Character matters because, without it, dealing with everything that life throws at all of us is much harder and only some succeed. For the individual, developing positive character traits gives them improved self-control, confidence and behaviour, which is expected to lead to better academic outcomes, improved employment outcomes and a better quality of life as well as a sense of personal flourishing.

The literature around character education also argues in favour of benefits to society such as better behaviour in school and in the community, greater civic responsibility and a more cohesive and stronger society. This could also be seen as offering more opportunities for social mobility, an answer to the divided society we've seen in recent years, and greater protection against problems such as radicalisation.

The demand for character development isn't found just amongst educators. In summer 2011 riots erupted across England. The reasons for the riots and the backgrounds of those taking part were many and various and in many cases the criminal actions of the rioters merited swift prosecutions and custodial sentences. But as the final report of the Riots Communities and Victims Panel[5] stated, "the key to avoiding future riots is to have communities that work" and part of that was, they believed, having communities "where parents and schools ensure children develop the values, skills and character to make the right choices at crucial moments".

In the final report, the Panel highlighted the importance of personal resilience, stating:

Many young people the Panel met expressed a sense of hopelessness. However, others, sometimes in the same school class, expressed optimism, self-sufficiency and a belief that their circumstances could be overcome.

5. webarchive.nationalarchives.gov.uk/20121003195937/http://riotspanel.independent.gov.uk/

We met people who had been convicted of all kinds of riot related offences. We also met many people who had suffered considerable disadvantage who had made a choice not to get involved in the riots. In asking what it was that made young people make the right choice in the heat of the moment, the Panel heard of the importance of character. A number of attributes together form character, including self-discipline, application, the ability to defer gratification and resilience in recovering from setbacks. Young people who develop character will be best placed to make the most of their lives.

In a similar vein, the UK Government's Drugs Strategy[6] states, "Schools have a key role to play in helping children and young people to develop the confidence and resilience needed to support academic attainment, to be valued by employers, and to make a positive contribution to British society. This means investing in a range of … programmes, which have a positive impact on young people … giving them confidence, resilience and risk management skills to resist risky behaviours and recover from set-backs."

> *For the individual, developing positive character traits gives them improved self-control, confidence and behaviour, which is expected to lead to better academic outcomes, improved employment outcomes and a better quality of life as well as a sense of personal flourishing.*

Those who say that character is not for schools to develop are often themselves working in school environments which are developing

---

6. www.gov.uk/government/uploads/system/uploads/attachment_data/file/628148/Drug_strategy_2017.PDF

character, but are doing so implicitly, and they haven't stopped to ask themselves what they are doing and why they aren't doing it deliberately. The fact that a pupil at such a school develops good character traits is more a happy accident than because of something taught deliberately to them. Isn't it better to be deliberate and explicit about how the environment we ask our teachers to work in and our students to study in is shaping their character and emphasising certain values and virtues?

A 2013 survey by the Jubilee Centre shows that parents want character to be taught. The poll showed:

- 87% of parents felt that schools should focus on character development and academic study, not simply academic study alone
- 84% of parents felt that teachers should encourage good morals and values in students
- 95% of parents felt that it is possible to teach a child values and shape their character in a positive sense, through lessons and dedicated projects or exercises at school
- 81% of parents wanted schools to have a core statement of the values that schools instilled in their pupils

We will look at the difference between explicit and implicit character education and whether it should be embedded in the wider curriculum or taught as a discrete topic in Chapter 9 but the Jubilee Centre in its 2017 Framework make no secret that schools should have a character education strategy, and the question to ask about that strategy "is not, therefore, whether such education does occur, but whether it is intentional, planned, organised, and reflective or assumed, unconscious, reactive and random".

This book calls for character to be deliberately developed by our schools and encourages schools to work within themselves and their local communities to identify the traits they want to develop. Addressing moral virtues is a hazardous occupation for politicians so I think the specific virtues to be developed are best left to each school and its community.

Performance and intellectual virtues are safer territory for policymakers and they fit better into the other policy areas we look at where having young people who demonstrate resilience, teamwork, confidence, reason and judgement or resourcefulness (to take the Jubilee Centre aspects) support broader nationwide objectives of having a skilled future workforce or promoting positive mental and physical wellbeing.

Character clearly means different things to many different people. My belief is that those engaged in education policy making should not try to define character explicitly or produce a list of virtues which all schools should be required to adopt and which can be reduced to a tick box list.

But everyone involved in our schools who believes in a broader purpose of education has a vested interest in ensuring our young people have certain key traits nurtured and developed to enable them to flourish at all ages and stages of their lives.

2

A ONE-NATION CHARACTER EDUCATION POLICY

❝❝ ONLY SOME

...why is it the case that only some of our schools, often in the independent sector, provide the necessary eco system to develop strong character traits?

❝❝ SOCIAL DIVISIONS

...in spite of 20 years of efforts by successive government to boost social mobility there are still too many divisions based on geography, income and generations in Britain.

❝❝ SOCIAL MOBILITY

My belief, though, is that we will fail to really turbocharge the social mobility which can be provided by education if we don't offer all pupils both a knowledge-rich, academically rigorous curriculum and the building of social capital.

❝❝ PRIVATE EDUCATION

...almost 7% of young people in England and Wales are privately educated and yet these students gain almost 50% of the total A and A* grades that are awarded each year.

❝❝ THE SUTTON TRUST

...the Sutton Trust's 2016 research...shows just how many of our leading judges, doctors, newspaper editors, top military personnel and politicians went to independent schools.

❝❝ ONE NATION

A one-nation character education policy means making it a clear requirement that every pupil, whatever their background, is entitled to be given the opportunity to develop both their knowledge and their character.

If we accept the argument that character education is essential for the full development of our young people, then, as I asked in the Introduction, why is it the case that only some of our schools, often in the independent sector, provide the necessary eco system to develop strong character traits? And they do this not at the expense of, but combined with, an excellent academic and rigorous education.

Jo Dibb, the Executive Headteacher of the outstanding Elizabeth Garrett Anderson School in Islington, London talks about the "confidence of class". Her belief is that her girls are going to need to be even better than their independent school rivals if they want to secure good jobs and bright futures because they start further behind. She talks of the school's role to "build social capital" and the school encouraging pupils to challenge their place in society as well as ensuring all pupils study an academically rigorous curriculum.

She actively compares her students to those studying at the nearby independent City of London School for Girls. Many of the pupils at Elizabeth Garrett Anderson come from what would be considered as disadvantaged backgrounds. The school cohort is diverse and many are working class Londoners.

In order to foster the skills needed everyone in the school has to "believe in excellence and raising aspirations". Teaching is conducted across year groups, which encourages pupils to act as role models and practise teamwork. There is an emphasis on growth mindset and reflective learning and everyone has to understand what they are expected to do in school.

Social and communication skills are treated as important and fostered through events such as formal lunches and dinners so that pupils are happy in different social settings. We all know that such social settings are essential for networking so it seems sensible to ensure pupils will be as comfortable as the girls from an independent school who are used to sitting around a table being full participants in the conversation.

The One-Nation Conservative political philosophy comes from the 19th century novel *Sybil, or The Two Nations* by Benjamin Disraeli, who became British Prime Minister in 1868. His novel was published in 1845. One-Nation Conservatives believe that societies exist and develop organically and that members within them have obligations to each other. Particularly important is the idea that those who are fortunate in life have obligations to the less advantaged parts of society. Britain is, even today, a hugely generous and charitable country. In the 2016 Charities Aid Foundation World Giving Index the UK was the eighth most generous nation in the world.

In his 1845 novel (which is still worth reading over 170 years later) Disraeli warned that Britain would become divided into two "nations" of the rich and poor as a result of increased industrialisation and inequality. If we replace the word 'industrialisation' with 'globalisation' then the post-June 2016 EU referendum arguments heard in Britain about a divided country show these themes have a huge resonance almost two centuries later.

> *Many of the reasons philanthropists and business people get involved in our education system as academy sponsors, trustees or governors is because they want to give something back.*

Many of the reasons philanthropists and business people get involved in our education system as academy sponsors, trustees or governors is because they want to give something back, extend to others the opportunities they had or, alternatively, to ensure the poor education they had is not suffered by others.

Education is often described as the great engine of social mobility. What is meant by that? Social mobility is about people being able to move between different social strata. This movement can be judged by earnings or occupation or living conditions such as housing.

The Social Mobility Commission is an advisory non-departmental public body. It has a duty to assess progress in improving social mobility in the UK and to promote social mobility in England. Its most recent, June 2017 report makes depressing reading with its finding that in spite of 20 years of efforts by successive governments to boost social mobility there are still too many divisions based on geography, income and generations in Britain. On a more optimistic note figures published in early 2017 show that income inequality has narrowed in Britain over the past 10 years as employment has increased.[7]

My belief, though, is that we will fail to really turbocharge the social mobility which can be provided by education if we don't offer all pupils both a knowledge-rich, academically rigorous curriculum and the building of social capital identified by the Head of Elizabeth Garrett Anderson School.

In *Schools for Human Flourishing*, Sir Iain Hall, the Chair of the Great Schools for All Children Trust, sets out the case for tackling the current unequal performance of our schools and pupils. He points out that almost 7% of young people in England and Wales are privately educated and yet these students gain almost 50% of the total A and A* grades that are awarded each year.

"With results such as these," Sir Iain says, "it is no surprise that

---

7. www.ons.gov.uk/peoplepopulationandcommunity/personalandhouseholdfinances/
incomeandwealth/bulletins/householddisposableincomeandinequality/financialyearending2016

approximately 45% of all Oxbridge entries come from the independent sector." This imbalance is backed up by the Sutton Trust's 2016 research report looking at the educational backgrounds of the nation's leading people[8] which shows just how many of our leading judges, doctors, newspaper editors, top military personnel and politicians went to independent schools.

As Sir Iain writes again, "It is clear that the 'privilege' of a child's parents being able to purchase an independent education can readily open more doors for their children than are open to their peers in the state sector." He continues:

There is little point, as educators, in being critical of wealth buying high quality education. Our challenge is to produce an education system which will raise the aspirations of all children and their families, drive their ambitions, address the lack of both intellectual and social capital that may be hindering the progress of those children, and empower them to break through the perceived glass ceiling of career progression so that there is social equity in terms of human flourishing.

Sir Iain helped to set up the King's Leadership in Warrington which was the overall winner of the first Department for Education Character Awards, a scheme I set up in 2015. He says that:

We knew that educating our young people to the same standards as the independent sector was to be our priority – but this could not happen unless we equipped them with the aspirations and strength of character to step out of their comfort zone and believe they could achieve. If we could achieve these two fundamental aims we would be empowering them to flourish and compete, at the end of their secondary education, with their peers from more advantaged circumstances. This led to 'educating, equipping and empowering' becoming the daily mantra which would drive us forward.

---

8. www.suttontrust.com/research-paper/leading-people-2016/

I was fortunate enough to visit King's Leadership Academy in early 2017 and it is a very impressive school with a clear vision of what it wants to achieve and how it intends to achieve it, as well as a clarity about what is expected of everyone, staff and students, who spend time there. There is a real 'can do' ethos and the school's motto is "Credimus" – "We believe". The words "Excellence is a Habit" loom large over the entrance hall and the school's clear mission statement is: "To develop in each of our students the academic skills, intellectual habits, quality of character and leadership traits necessary to succeed at all levels and become successful citizens in tomorrow's world."

At Gordano School in the South West of England pupils facing exclusion are referred to Sergeant Redrop, who joined the school thanks to the 'Troops to Teachers' scheme. Sergeant Redrop is employed as both a mentor and a PE teacher.

I didn't have the pleasure of meeting Sergeant Redrop when I visited the school but he had prepared for me a note of the strategies he had employed to pull five students back from becoming thoroughly disengaged from school. Building their characters through the interventions was the overall strategy.

He particularly mentioned Pupil A who had a twin and two older siblings and all of them had grown up with very limited paternal involvement. Pupil A is in receipt of pupil premium funding and has a special educational need. At home they experienced violence and neglect. Pupil A's twin had been permanently excluded from secondary school in Year 9, as had the eldest sibling. However, Pupil A was attending Army Cadets where they were flourishing and being a great role model for the younger cadets.

Sergeant Redrop had been in the Royal Marines and pointed out how that had enabled him to progress academically and as a person, "picking up those skills and qualities that are important in life". He continues:

Integrity, excellence, self-discipline and humility are all values that the Royal Marines hold dear and in turn these lead to courage, determination and unselfishness. Character can be built and indeed is, every moment we live. The decisions we make and experiences we

44

face give us character, we learn each time we take a path and adjust this each time we have the same or similar experience.

Students with Pupil A's background may not have as much opportunity as others to face this process and therefore fail to learn how to use criticism effectively, to see effort as a path to what they want and to embrace challenge successfully. These processes can see a person develop grit, resilience, intelligence, emotional intelligence, strength of mind, responsibility and empathy to name a few and these are characteristics we all want our pupils to gain.

The interventions employed to help Pupil A and four other pupils facing similar challenges include military-style personal training, mountain walking, following the positive example set by older pupils, visiting cadet forces and actively helping the pupils to plan their transition to college and sixth form. Tracking the attendance of the pupils and the penalties they received for poor behaviour showed that the number of penalties had fallen dramatically although attendance was still an "ongoing battle".

The conclusion Gordano has drawn from this intensive support and focus by one member of staff is that "mentoring and getting pupils to reflect on choices they make is an important part of this work and can reinforce to pupils that making the correct decision can mean a better relationship with teachers".

> *If we work hard, we can get a good education, achieve success and live lives better than those of previous generations.*

The important role schools and teachers have in successfully setting up a child for their future is not confined to the English school system.

Our Kids: The American Dream in Crisis by Robert D. Putnam has been a bestseller around the world. Of course it has particular resonance for its American audience but it asks some important questions which we can reflect on in Britain too. The idea of the book is that the promise of the American Dream is that anyone, regardless of where they start from, can have a fair start in life. If we work hard, we can get a good education, achieve success and live lives better than those of previous generations.

This is often referred to as the 'social contract' – meaning that the lives of future generations are better than those who have gone before us. Putnam identifies a disturbing 'opportunity gap' which has unexpectedly grown between kids from have and have-not backgrounds.

Critical to his research is the role of schools. Putnam asks whether schools in America today tend to widen the growing gaps between have and have-not kids; do they reduce those gaps or do they have little effect either way? We know that the single most important thing in improving the quality of teaching is ensuring the best teachers are in the classrooms. But the conclusion Putnam draws is that:

> Better teachers, who can have a substantial effect on student success in later life, are disproportionately found in upper-income, high-performance schools, whereas more transient, less capable teachers are disproportionately found in lower-income, low-performance schools. In short, poor teacher morale and higher turnover in low-income schools, driven by a climate of disorder and even danger, helps explain why low-income schools produce lower-achieving students, whatever the students' own background and ability.

A one-nation character education policy means making it a clear requirement that every pupil, whatever their background, is entitled to be given the opportunity to develop both their knowledge and their character. In the latter case, this means becoming literate about positive values and traits, being able to understand them and then being able to use them in the right circumstances, particularly when under pressure.

MENTAL RESILIENCE

💬 CHOICES

Today's young people, particularly girls, have more choices open to them than ever before so that, in itself, makes it harder to know what the right choice is.

💬 PUBLIC POLICY

If public policy makers know life is less certain and more complicated than it used to be, in many respects because of that uncertainty, then don't we have a duty to require our schools to help prepare their students for these uncertainties?

💬 WHOLE SCHOOL FOCUS

...as we see more and more young people reporting rising anxiety, depression, self-harm and behaviour problems then it is clear there must be a place for a whole school focus on wellbeing and resilience to help to address these issues.

💬 RESEARCH

Research in the resilience field suggests that individuals showing resilience are able to interact with their environment in ways that promote wellbeing or protect them against risk.

💬 COMFORT ZONE

I don't believe that we do young people any favours by stepping back from a knowledge-rich curriculum or helping them to avoid stressful situations such as exams or taking part in activities outside their comfort zone. But I do think that if we ask young people to do these things then those adults around them need to help them to develop the character to deal with those situations.

I s growing up harder in the 21st century than for previous generations? I was often asked this question when I visited schools during my time as Secretary of State. Or, sometimes, it wasn't a question but more a statement by those facing exams or the prospect of making career or future study choices.

I think it is an almost impossible question to answer. Today's young people, particularly girls, have more choices open to them than ever before so that, in itself, makes it harder to know what the right choice is. Rapid technological changes as well as the growth of social media are having a dramatic impact on school and home life. Future generations are competing for work and lifestyles not just with their peers in this country, but with the rest of the world. The next chapter looks at the role of character in providing the employees of the future.

> *Most of us would still much more happily confess to a physical illness than mental ill-health, however old we are.*

But I wanted to first look at mental resilience because I think that is of fundamental importance in preparing young people for life after education in the 21st century. Campaigns such as Time to Change and organisations such as YoungMinds, as well as brave young people who talk about their own mental health challenges, have helped reduce the stigma that being open about poor mental health carries. That doesn't mean the stigma is over – far from it. Most of us would still much more happily confess to a physical illness than mental ill-health, however old we are.

Many people working in this area prefer to use the term 'emotional health' which is probably broader than mental resilience but addresses the same need for individuals and society to possess the skills to deal with everything that life throws at them.

If public policy makers know life is less certain and more complicated than it used to be, in many respects because of that uncertainty, then don't we have a duty to require our schools to help prepare their students for these uncertainties?

Character education is not a preventative panacea for serious mental ill-health – there are times when there is no replacement for drugs and/ or therapy. But as we see more and more young people reporting rising anxiety, depression, self-harm and behaviour problems, it is clear there must be a place for a whole-school focus on wellbeing and resilience to help to address these issues. YoungMinds promotes an academic resilience programme which, as they say, "supports schools to step up the things they do so there is greater impact on the achievements of their most vulnerable or disadvantaged pupils." The link between wellbeing and results is explicitly made by YoungMinds and will be explored later. There are of course many other resources such as the Mindfulness in Schools Project.

Another approach is the Team of Life which uses sporting metaphors to encourage young people to recognise the strength and resilience in the people around them. Findings from a pilot project are discussed in an article by Vicky Eames, Catherine Shippen and Helen Sharp[9]. As they say, "Resilience, or the capacity to bounce back in the face of adversity,

9. shop.bps.org.uk/publications/educational-child-psychology-vol-33-no-2-june-2016-neuroscience-and-educational-psychology.html

is another concept that is considered to have important implications in the promotion of wellbeing. Research in the resilience field suggests that individuals showing resilience are able to interact with their environment in ways that promote wellbeing or protect them against risk".

They cite a paper by Bonnie Benard on fostering resilience published in 1991[10] saying "Young people who have high expectations, a meaning for life, goals, personal agency and interpersonal problem-solving skills are more likely to be resilient".

For the purposes of this book it is simply enough to note that these traits contribute to personal flourishing in a way which ultimately benefits not only the individual but their school and wider community. And, as this book argues, the development of those traits shouldn't be left to chance but should be deliberately developed by schools as part of their curriculum.

Steyning Grammar School in West Sussex wants "Every Person To Be the Best They Can Be". They say that although student results are important, the development of character strengths is equally important if their students are to flourish both at school and in their ongoing lives. Their approach is backed up by the field of Positive Psychology and they cite Dr Martin Seligman and the late Dr Chris Peterson who realised that "for people to become successful and happy – to flourish – they had to develop 24 character strengths". Steyning want character education to be at the core of what they do.

This work in the field of postive psychology was adapted by the KIPP schools in the USA and Dr Angela Duckworth to form a model that can be used in schools. This model focuses on the eight character strengths that most strongly underpin progression towards happy, engaged, meaningful and successful lives. These are: curiosity, zest, gratitude, grit, growth mindset, self control with learning, understanding others and self control with others.

---

10. files.eric.ed.gov/fulltext/ED335781.pdf

> *I don't believe that we do young people any favours by stepping back from a knowledge-rich curriculum or helping them to avoid stressful situations such as sitting exams or taking part in activities outside their comfort zone.*

The results from the pilot Team of Life project mentioned at the start of this chapter seemed to show a beneficial impact on promoting participants' confidence in achieving goals and "may have reduced some of the symptoms associated with the development of mental health and behavioural difficulties".

I don't believe that we do young people any favours by stepping back from a knowledge-rich curriculum or helping them to avoid stressful situations such as sitting exams or taking part in activities outside their comfort zone. But I do think that if we ask young people to do these things then those adults around them need to help them to develop the character to deal with those situations.

Mark Penney is Head of Solihull Junior School. The school has introduced specific resilience training to help his pupils develop "a skillset which will enable them to stay on track when the adversities of life might otherwise derail them. Helpfully the last couple of decades have seen a wealth of psychological research into the essence of human flourishing, providing us with a substantially better understanding of what helps children to thrive. So why wait for the wheels to fall off when positive psychology has given us a road map?"[11]

Many of those working in the fields of mental health and character or values education subscribe to the need for people to develop time for

---

11. *Private Schools* magazine, Autumn 2016

self-reflection. Mindfulness is becoming increasingly popular. Neil and Jane Hawkes of the Values-based Education Trust have developed what they call "Mindsight" – the ability to see one's own mind and sense those of others.

In *From My Heart: Transforming Lives Through Values*, Hawkes says, "the school curriculum generally focuses on facts, knowledge and skills related to the outside world, a material world that encourages children to concentrate their relationships on external objects – the external curriculum. Conversely, reflection focuses attention on the internal world of the brain and puts the spotlight on our relationship with our self and others – the internal curriculum."

And this use of reflection doesn't have to involve extra lessons or quiet time. Hawkes goes on to say:

Reflection can be used during any lesson. I watched a secondary school science teacher ask his class to stop their work, be still and reflect about what they were trying to achieve in the session. The quality of the lesson improved because of this pause.

Another example featured a humanities teacher, who had given her Year 11 students pieces of spiral-shaped pasta and asked them to look closely at each part of the spiral and, whilst observing, to reflect about why some people in the world were at the bottom of the spiral with very little, whilst others were at the top with so much. The richness of the debate that ensued, in terms of reasoning, was greatly enhanced by this reflective time.

Worth-it Projects is based in Loughborough and I have had the pleasure of working with them as their local MP. They make the link between mental health and character development clear:

Good character traits include persistence, the ability to work with others, humility and resilience in the face of failure. It is about being self-aware, being part of a community, selflessness and self-discipline. It is about playing a full role in society. However, good character is difficult to achieve with poor mental health. In order to build character you must address mental health and wellbeing and the earlier this is done the better for prevention and improved prospects for the future.

Schools are best placed to spot the early signs of poor mental health and emotional wellbeing and changes to the Ofsted common inspection framework has included the emotional and mental wellbeing of students – for schools to achieve good or outstanding status pupils must learn about emotional and mental health and be able to make informed choices regarding their emotional and mental wellbeing.

With the correct support and training schools can learn the techniques to identify mental health issues and in turn provide vulnerable young people with the tools to raise their mental wellbeing through building resilience – encouraging and support students to adapt during times of stress and adversity.

Let's return to the definition of education as set out in the Introduction, *ie* to lead or draw out that which lies within. If we can agree that education is about helping young people to flourish then that means helping them to develop, amongst other parts of their character, the resilience, including strong mental resilience and wellbeing, to cope with the many challenges of life in the 21st century.

4

DOES GRIT IMPROVE GRADES?

❝ POOR BEHAVIOUR

Poor behaviour and low-level disruption are the things which more teachers and pupils complain about than anything else. It is draining on teachers to keep having to tackle poor behaviour and it disrupts, very unfairly, the ability of other pupils to focus on the lessons.

❝ RESPONSIBILITY

It is clear that schools which focus on character work hard to ensure students accept responsibility for their attitude to their education. It seems to be the acceptance of responsibility and therefore the taking control of their education which leads students to do well.

❝ REFLECTION

…it requires each student to reflect on what they have done, what they enjoyed and found challenging and how the experience benefited them. The quality of their reflection is then commented on.

❝ INSTRUMENTAL

At every school I visited I asked the question of whether their character focus has improved or is expected to improve students' academic attainment. Every Headteacher believed that their character work was instrumental in students doing better and the school offering a better environment for students to learn in and staff to work in.

❝ POSITIVE OUTCOMES

The EEF believe there is good evidence that the skills such as self-control, self-perception, social skills, motivation and resilience underpin success in school and work and that someone who has those skills is more likely to have a positive outcome at school and later in life.

I n 2001 King's Langley School in Hertfordshire was in the bottom 3% of schools in England. By 2007/8 it was the second most improved in the country.

Haywood Academy which is based near Stoke-on-Trent had extremely poor results just four years ago in 2013. Now they are showing significant improvement. The primary school which has joined their City Learning Trust multi academy trust, Mill Hill Primary, has improved dramatically.

What happened at these schools to make the difference?

Gary Lewis, Head at King's Langley, firmly believes there is a link with character. When he arrived, Gary felt there was no 'cultural ethos' at the school. He wanted to see outstanding behaviour and outstanding morals so the first thing Gary did was to focus on improving behaviour.

Poor behaviour and low-level disruption are the things which more teachers and pupils complain about than anything else. It is draining on teachers to keep having to tackle poor behaviour and it disrupts, very unfairly, the ability of other pupils to focus on the lessons.

Gary Lewis knows that tackling poor behaviour made a huge difference in ensuring his pupils had the ability to study and learn. Now his staff will sometimes focus a lesson on how to concentrate – improving concentration being the lesson objective rather than anything else.

In order to demonstrate the character trait of 'stickability', students are given time to respond to feedback – through dedicated improvement and reflection time (otherwise known as DIRT). Staff are expected to build this time into their lessons so students have to look at their own work and reflect about what they have done and what they could do to improve it.

Carl Ward, Head at Haywood Academy, says that character does improve results. He believes that improving results in subjects such as maths and English, important though they are, only gets a school so far. He believes that if a school builds character "then [pupils] can move through situations with confidence".

Carl believes that students have to "get used to handling the pressure" so they take 'exams' every six weeks.

Babington College in Leicester serves a very disadvantaged and diverse community. At Babington they focus on 'BCL' – building character for learning. When asked about the impact on academic attainment the school says it is hard to isolate which intervention has worked best for their pupils but they firmly believe, given the background of many of the pupils, that they need to be "emotionally equipped for learning" and building resilience is key to success. BCL objectives are displayed on the board at the start of each lesson, and language to build and reinforce the need for stamina is used throughout the lesson.

In *Schools for Human Flourishing*, Patsy Kane, Executive Headteacher at the Education and Learning Trust, and Elizabeth Hole, Academy Headteacher at Whalley Range 11-18 High School, write, "Confidence and self-belief are key aspects of achieving strong academic results. Students needed to grow their resilience in learning as they had in their personal lives."

> *It seems to be the acceptance of responsibility and therefore the taking control of their education which leads students to do well.*

It is clear that schools which focus on character work hard to ensure students accept responsibility for their attitude to their education. It seems to be the acceptance of responsibility and therefore the taking control of their education which leads students to do well.

At Gordano School, near Bristol, Headteacher Gary Lewis asked a senior member of staff, Peter Morris, to look at why high-achieving students did so well. Morris's conclusion was that it was because those students wanted to do well. The challenge then for the leadership team was to work out what they had to do to ensure all the other students wanted to do well too.

The school worked out what they call a "taxonomy of effort" which forms the basis of every student profile. The Gordano School Effort profile sets out six ways to measure effort and four levels of judging how great an effort has been made. The six measurements are: resilience, independence, self-management, response to feedback, response to challenge and response to setbacks.

So, a level 1 judgement for resilience states that a student "always shows keenness and commitment to succeed, has excellent concentration and is rarely off task". But a level 4 judgement (the lowest category) states that a student is judged to have "frequent and/or sustained pauses in learning and shows little interest in their learning and poor completion of tasks".

A level 4 judgement for response to setbacks states the student is "inclined to give up when setbacks occur" whereas a level 1 judgement states the student "actively learns from setbacks and mistakes".

Each student then has their own Learner Profile on an online system called Reflect. The Learner Profile is described as:

...a tool to help you:

- *Reflect on your development as a learner and become a better learner as a result*
- *Build a picture of your skills development*

- *Build a picture of your involvement in a wide range of activities, both in and out of school*

It will also help you to:

- *Make choices about the future based on an understanding of your strengths*
- *Prepare yourself for some of the challenges you will face when eventually you leave Gordano*

Gordano Reflect makes it clear that students will focus on the following sections of the Learner Profile as they move through the school:

Year 7 – Your Mindset
Year 8 – Your Personal Learning and Thinking Skills
Year 9 – Your Mindset and Your Employability
Year 10 – Your Personal Learning and Thinking Skills and
            Your Employability
Year 11 – Your Mindset and Your Employability
Year 12 – Your Personal Qualities and Your Employability
Year 13 – Your Personal Qualities and Your Employability

In common with many other schools which pride themselves on the character development of their students, Gordano seems to be always open to new activities and wants students to be open in the same way. They therefore offer the Gordano Guarantee – nine experiences promised to each and every student:

- Go on a residential visit
- Perform to an audience or represent the school or your house
- Visit the theatre or attend a professional performance
- Meet people who have achieved something extraordinary
- Engage in an international project
- Visit a place of historic or cultural importance
- Belong to a club, society or team
- Take part in a week's work experience
- Actively support a charity or help your community

The important thing though about the Gordano Reflect system is not just that it records what each student is doing or allows a member of staff to make a judgement about the effort used, but it requires each student to reflect on what they have done, what they enjoyed and found challenging and how the experience benefited them. The quality of their reflection is then commented on.

Gordano's Head, Gary Lewis, firmly believes that reflection builds character and allows everyone to learn from their mistakes and the things they found difficult. He also talks about this practice of allowing students to find the language which enables them to put their experiences into words and this helps them be more articulate generally.

Having a growth mindset is important at Gordano and, as can be seen from the Learner Profile, encouraging each student to focus on their mindset and reflect on how they demonstrate the key attitudes of having a growth mindset is part of the school's character development work. At assemblies, Gary will make it clear that, as far as he is concerned, "the most important thing is how the students develop as people."

> *Staff are expected to take on extracurricular activities in order to role model their service to the students.*

Staff at Gordano receive their own training on mindset and Gary talks about values in the staff daily briefing. Staff are expected to take on extracurricular activities in order to role model their service to the students.

Gordano is currently rated as 'Outstanding' by Ofsted, has an above national average Progress 8 score and the percentage of pupils getting a Grade C or above in English and maths GCSEs has risen from 62% in 2014 to 79% in 2016.

At Elizabeth Garett Anderson School in North London, the all-female student cohort is taught across the years which provides mentoring and role model opportunities. Again a growth mindset and reflective learning culture is fostered and students are awarded 'commitment to learning' grades. They are specifically told what is expected of them.

At Tapton School in Sheffield, the focus is on "learning behaviours". Students are expected to demonstrate five key behaviours – resilience, resourcefulness, reflectiveness, reciprocity and respect, values and attitude. There are nine levels of ability so they can demonstrate moving from a level 1 which is "dependent, disorganised but willing" to a level 9 which is "outstanding level of independence – an accomplished and sophisticated and learner". For example a level 9 student practising resilience will behave as follows:

Sets and modifies goals to suit the context of their learning. Always maintains concentration and engagement across a sequence of lessons, however challenging. Prepared to put off immediate short term gain for greater long term success.

A level 1 student practising resilience will, by contrast, behave as follows:

Periodic engagement with learning. Responds to motivation from the teacher inconsistently.

Tapton's learning behaviours are tracked three times a year and were introduced in September 2014 as the school evolved from an "approach to learning" model to the current learning behaviours. Staff at Tapton are used to innovating and to what they call Tapton Learning Communities. They are each set a teaching and learning pledge for the academic year and lessons can be filmed and watched by the staff members so they are able to reflect on the lesson they have taught.

The learning behaviours are reinforced through posters around the school, assemblies, PSHE lessons, parents evenings and staff training. In the words of Executive Headteacher David Dennis, everyone at the school "has to live" this approach inside and outside the classroom.

Growth mindset parents' evenings are held for families with students in Years 7, 10 and 12 and evenings are held for Year 6 parents who have children hoping to join the school. Feedback to students has to be "positive, critical and formative" and they receive a rating on "where they are as a learner". David Dennis talks about the students becoming "desensitised to failure" because of the feedback they receive and their self-reflections.

Villiers Park is an educational charity based in Cambridgeshire which runs a scholars programme for bright post-16 kids from disadvantaged backgrounds who aren't achieving the best results they should. They describe themselves as a national social mobility charity stating, "We set out to address all the obstacles that prevent success. By success we mean achieving the confidence, key skills and examination results needed to gain access to a top university or other centre of excellence, to thrive once there and to embark on a successful career."

They would admit it is hard to measure their success but in 2016 their results told a very impressive story:

Year 11

- 17% of grades were A* (against a national average of 6.5%)
- 32% of grades were A (against a national average of 14%)
- 80% of grades were A*-B (against a national average of 42%)
- 95% of grades were A*-C (against a national average of 67%)

Year 13

- 41% of A level grades were A*-A (against a national average of 26%)
- 63% of A level grades were A*-B (against a national average of 53%)
- 82% of scholars gained a place at university (against a national average of 32% for all 18-year-olds; 46% from the most advantaged backgrounds; 19% from the most disadvantaged backgrounds)

Surveys of scholars in Year 11 found that their programme has had a positive effect on their...

Communication skills – 100%	Resilience – 91%
Enthusiasm for learning – 97%	Research – 91%
Self-confidence – 97%	Grade attainment – 88%
Ability to work in a team – 97%	

Surveys of scholars in Year 13 found that their programme has had a positive effect on their...

Communication skills – 96%	Ability to work in a team – 92%
Choice of university – 96%	What job/career to pursue – 84%
Resilience – 92%	Enthusiasm for learning – 80%
Self-confidence – 92%	

One hundred per cent of the parents of Year 11 and Year 13 scholars surveyed indicated that the programme had a positive effect on their child, improving their confidence, resilience, enthusiasm for learning, communication, aspirations and ambitions. As we will see from the example set by West Midlands primary, St James Church of England in Stourbridge, feedback from parents is an important part of assessing the benefits of character education.

And, for Villiers Park scholars, the benefits don't stop when they leave school. Importantly, their alumni survey of 2016 graduates showed fantastic results:

- 99% retention for the duration of their course (against a national average of 94%)
- 95% of scholars graduated with a 1st or 2:1 (against a national average of 73% for all students)
- 86% of students from low income backgrounds attended a leading university (100% of those attending a leading university graduated)

At King's Leadership Academy, Warrington, students have five assessments per year. At their final assessment, any failings will be picked up, discussed and then the student is expected to reflect and move on. The Academy believes in students conducting lots of self-evaluation in order to practise being self-aware, correcting their behaviour and then being able to move on to the next situation or challenge.

One of the educational beliefs at King's Leadership Academy is that "uncorrected learning errors are responsible for most young people's learning difficulties". The assessments mentioned above are held as much to discover what students don't yet know. After each assessment a week is set aside in which staff ensure any gaps in knowledge are filled and all errors or misconceptions are corrected.

Although the values at King's Leadership Academy are broader than just being related to how students learn, a key value is self-awareness and this is encouraged by a real focus on self-reflection on not only a student's lessons but also their creative involvements and activities such as residential trips they have completed.

Another part of the King's Leadership ethos is that each student should follow the REACH methodology in their work – research, explore, analyse, create and hypothesise. The school practises enquiry-based learning and at the start of each Learning Cycle students are set a "challenging question" in every subject.

At every school I visited I asked the question of whether their character focus has improved or is expected to improve students' academic attainment. Every Headteacher believed that their character work was instrumental in students performing better and the school offering a better environment for students to learn in and staff to work in.

In order to get some substantive evidence to support this Head's instinct, the UK Education Endowment Foundation (EEF) has, at the time of writing, launched 18 research projects that relate to character skills. The trials are reaching over 1000 schools and 65,000 pupils. Sixty per cent are whole-class interventions, involving teacher training, and the other projects are split between whole-school and targeted approaches.

The EEF believe there is good evidence that the skills such as self-control, self-perception, social skills, motivation and resilience underpin success in school and work and that someone who has those skills is more likely to have a positive outcome at school and later in life.

The EEF research is designed to understand how skills can be developed and what works in doing this. In terms of interventions, the EEF state that the evidence is probably strongest in relation to social and emotional learning programmes.

Average effect sizes of social and emotional learning interventions on attainment are equivalent to an extra four months' progress. Other interventions which the EEF believe could be promising include extracurricular activities that have links to classroom learning (including social action), engaging parents in children's early learning and approaches that encourage children to reflect on their learning and interact with others.

Because the UK evidence base is still limited it is worth looking overseas and one of the most relevant studies dates from America in 2003[12]. This study by Benninga, Berkowitz, Kuehn and Smith looked at "the relationship of character education implementation and academic achievement in elementary schools". The results did indicate that "a composite summary score of character education criteria is positively correlated with academic indicators across years. The elementary schools in [the] sample with solid character education programmes ... not only show positive relationships with academic indicators that same year, but also evidence positive correlations across the next two academic years". Their final conclusion is that "those schools addressing the character education of their students in a serious, well-planned manner tended also to have higher academic achievement scores".

Perhaps the better evidence is, as Shane Ierston from King's Leadership Academy, suggested, through proxy measures such as reduced absence and better behaviour as well as greater student, parent and staff satisfaction.

---

12. www.csufresno.edu/kremen/bonnercenter/documents/Character_Education.pdf

This was supported by Sally Sixsmith, the Head at St James Church of England Primary School in Stourbridge in the West Midlands. St James was rated as 'Requires Improvement' in 2013 and one of the factors cited by inspectors was that pupils were found to be too passive about their learning and needed to take greater responsibility.

Working on that, and putting in place their clear focus on values, meant that when I asked Sally and her Deputy Head, Lindsay, for their view on my question they also pointed to proxy measures. Those they mentioned included reported incidents of bullying being down every year, reports on poor behaviour being down, their pupils being able to de-escalate situations which might turn into an argument, attendance being up and the fact that there had been a positive impact on homework and reading at home.

Perhaps just as importantly, when, after the first year of really focusing on values, they asked parents if they had noticed a difference in their children, the feedback from parents was extremely positive.

Of course external bodies such as Ofsted play a role too given the requirement for them to pass judgement on a school's social, moral, spiritual and cultural record. As Ofsted said in December 2014 about King's Langley, Hertfordshire, "The headteacher and senior leaders have created a school in which students learn to develop the qualities of character and the academic skills to become successful citizens ... Students make good progress across a wide range of subjects. This is because they have excellent attitudes to learning. They learn not to give up and to support each other."

5

ADULT ROLE MODELS

" SCHOOL LEADERS

...for really successful character development the lead has to come from the top of the school. The role of school leaders in creating a school of character cannot be underestimated.

" EXHIBIT VALUES

...even those schools, or individuals within them, which claim not to have the desire or time to focus on character education do exhibit values which their pupils will pick up.

" SCHEMES

...things such as badges, rewards and being part of a House or group are important in developing character traits and, of course, the simple act of having such schemes in itself sets the school's ethos such as rewarding good behaviour or qualities such as perseverance or the importance of teamwork.

" VALUES-BASED SCHOOL

Becoming a values-based school requires everyone involved, staff, pupils,parents and community to identify the values they want to promote and adopt and then to identify behaviours which will model the values.

" TEACHER TRAINING

If we want character education to be embedded within our curriculum and practised in our schools then it needs to be included in teacher training and explicitly developed and recognised in the assessment of trainee teachers.

Some of the most important role models in the lives of our young people are their teachers, in particular those in leadership positions. If we are talking about the need for adults to model character traits and values then clearly the most important places outside the family home in terms of developing character are our schools.

From my observations and the many, many school visits I made as Secretary of State, and continue to make as a local MP, the schools with the strongest values culture, where everyone subscribes to those values, aims to model them and to challenge those who fall short, are the most successful, the most cohesive and where pupils really flourish.

But for really successful character development the lead has to come from the top of the school. The role of school leaders in creating a school of character cannot be underestimated.

In *Teaching Character in the Primary Classroom*, Harrison, Morris and Ryan say that school leaders have to do the following:

- Be visible champions for character education
- Help teachers understand that the greatest influence on the pupils' character is their own character
- Ensure that all teachers are adequately trained to critically reflect on and convey character education to their pupils
- Initially take the leadership role in the development of a character-centred mission statement and ensure this is regularly reviewed

As Paul Tough says in *How Children Succeed*, "If it's not woven into the DNA of an institution it will have minimal impact." So, even those schools, or individuals within them, which claim not to have the desire or time to focus on character education do exhibit values which their pupils will pick up.

Professor James Arthur says in *Of Good Character*:

Through its very existence, every educational institution already models a set of values to its pupils by means of the relations between staff, staff and pupils, organisation and discipline. It is far better that this process be a conscious one, rationally organised, so that it becomes possible to evaluate what the school is saying, how it says it, and hopefully to monitor the outcomes of the process.

In the same book, Arthur sets out his research into the influences on the lives of young people. He writes, "Teachers are perceived to be moral authorities by their pupils, whatever they themselves might think about their teaching." He cites Professor A H Halsey who said in his 1994 work *The Transformation of Society* that, "teaching has largely been reduced to an academic transaction between old and young people which nowadays eschews responsibility for the really difficult part of developing character in the young." Arthur continues, "[Halsey] believes that present day teachers need to take the 'parenting' role more seriously insofar as education has the deeper purpose of teaching people how to live well."

Arthur's research, which was published in 2003 in *Of Good Character*, reports...

Important influences in the lives of young people

The following people helped develop my character	% who agreed
Mother	82
Father	69
Friends	57
Siblings	52
Teachers	48
Grandparents	46
Other family	39
People in media	23
Community leaders	21

Arthur goes on to say:

Schooling is unavoidably a moral enterprise. Indeed, schools teach morality in a number of ways, both implicit and explicit. It should be noted, though, that very few schools feature 'moral education' as a discrete and acknowledged subject within the curriculum. Instead, schools have a moral ethos embodied in rules, rewards and punishments, dress codes, relationships, styles of teaching, sports and in the levels of respect evident in teacher-pupil associations. Schools convey to children what is expected of them, what is normal, what is right and wrong. It is often claimed that values are caught rather than taught; it is through their ethos, that schools socialise children into patterns of moral behaviour.

Of course, Arthur's work and research in this field (and he is now the Director of the Birmingham University Jubilee Centre for Character and Virtues) has led to him being a driving force behind the University of Birmingham School where they are able to put into practice the link between school, education and the development of character and virtues in the pupils.

Chapter 9 examines how individual schools create the moral ethos Arthur talks about and how they approach character education. It will be seen that things such as badges, rewards and being part of a House or group are important in developing character traits and, of course, the simple act of having such schemes in itself sets the school's ethos such as rewarding good behaviour or qualities such as perseverance or the importance of teamwork.

Dr Neil Hawkes from the Values-based Education Trust is clear that role modelling is given a high priority in values-based secondary schools worldwide. He says in his book *From My Heart: Transforming Lives Through Values*:

> Being a role model for children means being the sort of person you hope they will want to become ... We model what it is to be a values-based human being. How we model this will, to a large degree determine what a child thinks they should grow up to be. This is why I consider that parents, and also adults who work in schools are very important for the creation of a civil society. They are in the forefront of positive, cultural transformation. In turn, the children become role models too.

Becoming a values-based school requires everyone involved – staff, pupils, parents and community – to identify the values they want to promote and adopt and then to identify behaviours which will model the values. This can be a tricky conversation for staff to have because each will have a different teaching style and way of behaving – we all do. Hawkes says that a values-based culture is one that is "calm and purposeful, and where there is mutual respect." The purpose of a staff conversation is to ensure there is consistency in the school. For students to take the school's values seriously, they need to feel that each member of staff will treat them according to the school's values.

Hawkes has identified that if this works well it creates a more positive environment for the staff themselves to work in. It seems ultimately impossible to work in an environment which requires the adults to model respect, tolerance, integrity and to think about developing strong character traits in their pupils without that rubbing off on staff relationships too, although I am sure some schools do try and then wonder why their approach does not stick.

Sergeant Redrop, who works at Gordano School to mentor particularly challenging pupils who are most at risk of exclusion, was mentioned earlier. He is clear that many children gather character qualities:

...from those they are surrounded by as they grow up, mothers, fathers, brothers, sisters and many other role models that pass in and out of their lives. The pupils we are surrounded by every day, pick up more from teachers than we can ever imagine, this coupled with the fact that some of these pupils have no father and in rare cases no mother. As male teachers, it is our job to be a role model for these pupils guiding them in a direction that is in synchronization with life outside the school gates.

At Gordano role modelling is done not just by the staff but also by more senior pupils within the school. Sixth form students are able to dedicate some of their free time to help younger pupils with their work. This support includes helping pupils prepare for exams by showing them how to take effective notes in class and revise.

Sergeant Redrop is clear that pupils will always look up to those closest to them. He believes this is how teachers, who have developed positive character traits, can help to guide pupils away from other adults "whose character can sometimes be brought into question".

> *We all know that all schools are not the same, but rather than leaving it to a hunch at interview for new members of staff, a school's values and their approach to developing good character should be explicitly stated and discussed and the candidate asked to give their views on this.*

Character, and particularly a school's values and the way in which they are developed in their pupils, should be a part of any staff interview process. We all know that all schools are not the same, but rather than leaving it to a hunch at interview for new members of staff, a school's values and their approach to developing good character should be explicitly stated and discussed and the candidate asked to give their views on this.

At Gordano School, one of the key interview questions for potential new members of staff is to ask for views on whether hard work is a virtue. King's Leadership Academy in Warrington are clear that personal values and integrity are specifically tested at staff interviews. St James Primary in Stourbridge are clear that values are part of their interview process for middle management and that every member of staff must be a role model for the school's values.

If we want character education to be embedded within our curriculum and practised in our schools then it needs to be included in teacher training and explicitly developed and recognised in the assessment of trainee teachers. It also needs to be reflected and enhanced in ongoing *continuing professional development* for teachers.

Every school already has its own character and models a set of values to students and staff consciously and unconsciously. In the same way that character can be both caught and taught, it can be built through targeted instruction and also embedded in everyday classroom practice. Research shows though that either way most character education is teacher-led.

Examples of embedding character education in everyday classroom practice include through behaviour sanctions and rewards, through pedagogy, through the teacher's own behaviour and modelling and by exploring character in the context of the curriculum.

Targeted teaching methods include extracurricular activities such as sport or community service, dedicated teaching on performance virtues such as growth mindset or teaching metacognitive strategies or through ethics or specific character lessons. Explicit recording or reporting of character is another way of specifically targeting character development work and is likely to be monitored and checked by teaching staff.

> *Teacher training simply has to catch up and cover the development of pupils' character (and therefore their own) in sufficient depth so that the enthusiasm of the trainee teacher for character development is stimulated and does not fall away.*

But despite the key role of teachers in this vital area, in terms of both teaching positive character traits as well as modelling them, it is widely acknowledged that there is currently a lack of adequate training. Research has shown that many teachers consider the moral dimensions of education more important than academic success and many enter teaching expecting to be moral agents. Teacher training simply has to catch up and cover the development of pupils' character (and therefore their own) in sufficient depth so that the enthusiasm of the trainee teacher for character development is stimulated and does not fall away.

The teaching of character to future teachers can be achieved by teaching both the theory as well as suggested classroom practice, including the identification of the necessary values language so that teachers can use that language confidently and accurately to address ethical issues in the classroom.

There is a debate about the extent to which character education teacher training needs to be an explicit and distinct part of teacher training. There are those who advocate minimalist strategies which would focus on making clear the hidden moral curriculum and encouraging teachers to reflect upon this in their ordinary practice.

Others advocate maximalist strategies where teachers would learn a toolkit of pedagogical strategies that target character directly as a curricular goal. It is, however, important that this maximalist teaching is practical and based on real and effective classroom practice. The growth of teacher training in schools lends itself to achieving this.

Of course, successful teacher training doesn't end when a trainee leaves initial teacher training. Almost every school I visited talked with great enthusiasm about the ongoing training on character and virtues which they provide to their staff.

At King's Leadership, what happens, in terms of leadership and character development, for the pupils takes place for staff too. Ninety minutes is set aside on Fridays for staff training. The school is clear that staff training is constant and regard it as their investment in their staff. On Wednesday mornings there are 20-minute pedagogy briefings and different leadership strategies in different companies are examined.

Staff can take qualifications with the Institute of Character and Leadership which has links with the Chartered Management Institute. Staff will carry out "mastery, autonomy and purpose" (known as MAP) projects which lead to a CMI qualification.

CPD is also emphasised at Haywood Academy where the view is that "character creates soul and soul comes from the staff". It is noticeable, says Head Carl Ward, that they do attract staff more easily than other schools. Who wouldn't want to work in an organisation that wants to invest in its staff?

The link between home environment and school is always important, but particularly important is the consistency needed to reinforce at home the character messages emphasised at school. That is why it is vital to involve parents and the wider community in identifying the values and virtues to be instilled in the first place.

In Chapter 9 we examine how some schools bring parents into the process of identifying the character traits they are going to prioritise. But it is clear that the primary shaping of a child's character comes from the parents. Although school plays an important part, children can and do revert to old behaviours when away from the school environment. So, for improvement in behaviour and the development of key character traits to 'stick', and be long lasting, parental buy-in is crucial.

As Paul Tough says, "When parents get the support they need to create a warm, stable, nurturing environment at home, their children's stress levels often go down, while their emotional stability and psychological resilience improve."

How do parents get the necessary support? In the case of character education there seem to be three core types of parental intervention. In the early years arena, interventions could be carried out via intensive home visiting or day care designed to provide neurological development and promote good parenting. The second type of intervention is the programmes which encourage strong emotional health in children and parents, and promote good parenting.

The final type of interventions can be grouped together under the 'collaborative improvement' banner. These are the kinds of initiatives from schools designed to involve parents in children's school life and development. For example, at King's Leadership, parents attend the school's ASPIRE ceremony where their child is formally inducted into the school. The induction explicitly reinforces the importance of this character aspect. Tapton School in Sheffield holds growth mindset evenings for the parents of pupils in Years 7, 10 and 12.

King's Langley give presentations to parents on student leadership. They have also held character sessions for parents, challenging them to debate and decide how they would handle situations involving their children where good character traits are most needed. Head Gary Lewis recounts that these sessions have led to some passionate debates amongst parents and they are a real reflection of different parenting styles!

As Steve Harris of Wellbeing Education points out, "The great news about ... character work is that it can give parents a real opportunity to focus on aspects of their child's personality that they value, and would like to strengthen. It can also be used as a vehicle for *creating* greater engagement in learning with parents, who may feel more confident with the language of your characteristics than the ever shifting landscape of teaching methodology."

He recommends, as we will consider in Chapter 9, that parents meetings are held to launch any character discussion if this is a new departure for a school. Many parents feel unable to really get to grips about the curriculum their child faces but "explicitly knowing that completing [homework] in the face of all the other tempting distractions is an exercise in self-control, and that this in turn is a strong predictor for future success, gives the whole exercise a greater sense of purpose. And self-control, like other characteristics, is something that gets better with sustained effort."

> *Having those values discussed and consistently referred to and reinforced at both school and home is important, but it is clear there is no substitute for influential adults role modelling those values and traits too and not just talking about them.*

Everyone – teacher, senior leader, parent or pupil – needs to be constantly reminded of the importance of strong values which underpin their character. Having those values discussed and consistently referred to and reinforced at both school and home is important, but it is clear there is no substitute for influential adults role modelling those values and traits too and not just talking about them.

6

PREPARING FOR THE
WORKPLACE

❝ MOST OF US

...unless a person is born with a trust fund the fact is that most of us have to get a job and plan our careers and working lives.

❝ SOFT SKILLS

To thrive in today's workplaces our students need not just knowledge and qualifications but other skills, often referred to as "soft" or "non-cognitive" skills. Character education or personal development as the CBI refer to it in their 2016 skills survey has an important role to play.

❝ ATTITUDES AND ATTRIBUTES

Businesses are clear that first and foremost they want to recruit young people with attitudes and attributes such as resilience, enthusiasm and creativity. They are not selecting simply on the basis of academic ability.

❝ EVIDENCE THESE SKILLS

One of the key recommendations was that "Non-cognitive skills and attributes such as team working, emotional maturity, empathy, and other interpersonal skills are as important as proficiency in English and mathematics in ensuring young people's employment prospects". They recommended that the assessment system find a way to evidence these skills.

❝ HIGHER–SKILLED JOBS

...as many low-skilled positions are replaced by machines, the higher-skilled jobs being created will require greater manual dexterity or greater cognitive skills such as those that depend on management or human social interaction.

E ducation is not all about getting young people ready for a job. It is about gathering knowledge about the world we live in, identifying strengths, broadening horizons, developing as a person and, of course, gaining formal qualifications. But unless a person is born with a trust fund, the fact is that most of us have to get a job and plan our careers and working lives.

And in the 21st century, there is no such thing as a job for life. Many of today's pupils will have up to eight different careers during their working lives. As one of my predecessors, Estelle Morris, has pointed out, we are asking completely different things of our education system now than we did 100 years ago or more. Then, basic literacy and numeracy was enough for most school leavers to have gained. Only those from the top echelons of society, and then usually only if they were men, went on to study at a higher level.

To thrive in today's workplaces, our students need not just knowledge and qualifications but other skills, often referred to as "soft" or "non-cognitive" skills. Character education (or personal development as the CBI refer to it in their 2016 Skills Survey) has an important role to play.

The CBI's 2016 Skills Survey[13] says:

It is essential that all young people get the support they need in our schools and colleges to fulfil their potential – and businesses rely on schools to help young people develop the attributes and knowledge

13. www.cbi.org.uk/cbi-prod/assets/File/pdf/cbi-education-and-skills-survey2016.pdf

80

that will enable them to succeed in their working lives. This means developing key skills and knowledge in combination with the attitudes and behaviours needed for success in life and work. Stretching academic standards alone are not sufficient.

Businesses are clear that first and foremost they want to recruit young people with attitudes and attributes such as resilience, enthusiasm and creativity. They are not selecting simply on the basis of academic ability.

Our survey results show the overwhelming importance of young people's attitudes to work in determining their job prospects and future success. More than four out of five employers (89%) rate this as one of their three most important considerations. It consistently ranks far ahead of every other factor by a wide margin. The CBI has long pointed to the central importance of a positive attitude and resilience, demonstrated for example by a readiness to take part, openness to new ideas and activities, and a desire to achieve. This attitude also involves understanding that hard work and effort yield results.

Also ranking ahead of formal results and qualifications are young people's aptitudes for work (cited as important by 66%). Core skills such as basic literacy and numeracy (37%) are also more important than academic results or formal qualifications obtained (cited by 36% and 23% respectively as among the three most important factors). One in five businesses also view business awareness and relevant work experience as among the three top considerations when recruiting young people (21% and 20% respectively).

… More than a third of businesses (37%) report they are not satisfied with school and college leavers' attitudes to work. This is a troubling finding, given that this is the single most important consideration when young people are seeking that critical first job opening. Almost as concerning is the finding that nearly half (48%) of businesses are not satisfied with the resilience and self-management of young people, while more than a quarter (26%) report poor teamworking skills. These are capacities needed for virtually every job in every sector …

... In terms of skills and capabilities, businesses want to see schools ensuring that young people master the essentials. Businesses see it as a priority for schools to help pupils develop the effective communication skills that are so essential in personal and working life (a top-three priority for 38% of respondents). Enabling young people to develop self-management and appropriate personal behaviour (37%) is another important aim. Qualities such as resilience and the capacity to focus are important both for future learning and success in any work environment. Unless these become firmly embedded during their time at school, it will be hard for young people to thrive later in life.

In January 2014 Professor Sir Roy Anderson chaired an Advisory Group for Pearson on 'Making Education Work'. One of the key recommendations was that "Non-cognitive skills and attributes such as teamworking, emotional maturity, empathy, and other interpersonal skills are as important as proficiency in English and mathematics in ensuring young people's employment prospects". They recommended that the assessment system find a way to evidence these skills.

Anyone reading this book who is an employer or who has interviewed applicants for a job will know that those candidates able to demonstrate self-confidence (not arrogance, which is immensely off putting), empathy, continued curiosity and a willingness to learn and the ability to work as part of a team scores highly even if they might need more on-the-job training.

There isn't space in this book to open up another complex issue, namely careers advice, but when I was Secretary of State I was pleased to be able to oversee the setting up and investing in the Careers and Enterprise Company. The Careers and Enterprise Company exists to help young people transition from education to employment by assisting them to develop the insights, understanding and skills that will lead to them building a career. The Company believes in students having multiple opportunities to learn from employers about work, employment and the skills that are valued in the workplace. This can be through a range of enrichment activities including visiting speakers, mentoring and enterprise schemes.

One of the other issues in today's workplaces which needs to be addressed is recognised in a recent Deloitte report entitled 'From Brawn to Brains: the impact of technology on jobs in the UK'. The report makes clear that as many low-skilled positions are replaced by machines, the higher-skilled jobs being created will require greater manual dexterity or greater cognitive skills such as those that depend on management or human social interaction.

Therefore it is absolutely critical that young people should develop those skills necessary to enable them to survive and flourish in the 21st century workplace.

Workplace skills aren't solely confined to literacy or numeracy or knowledge or expertise. Employers are saying very clearly, in survey after survey, that broader non-cognitive skills are missing. I would argue that as well as embedding those skills in a school curriculum they can also be explicitly developed by schools and teachers.

7

ASSESSING CHARACTER

WHAT GETS ASSESSED

One of Whitehall's favourite mantras is "What gets assessed, gets done". I suspect it is one of the education system's least favourite mantras but, given the public investment in our education system, it is in everyone's interest to know how pupils are doing.

MEASUREMENTS

If measurement is desired then would we measure each child's character or, rather, the schools' efforts and programmes to develop character?

ASKING QUESTIONS

Simply asking the questions about character traits and development will focus minds on the importance of this and the priority given to it by a school and its leadership.

UNINTENDED CONSEQUENCES

The risk with designing an assessment system for character is that it can drive perverse behaviour and lead to unintended consequences.

OFSTED

Of course if character is being either specifically taught or included with the broader curriculum then the school leadership and outside agencies such as Ofsted could assess the teaching to ensure they do reflect the traits and values each school has identified as important.

One of Whitehall's favourite mantras is, "What gets assessed, gets done." I suspect it is one of the education system's least favourite mantras but, given the public investment in our education system, it is in everyone's interest to know how pupils are doing. Are they literate and numerate? How are schools performing? Are lessons outstanding or in need of improvement?

When I was in the Department for Education and working out our priorities after the 2015 General Election, I was clear that focusing on character education should be one of them. But how would we measure what progress had been made in developing students' character and what does character education success look like?

As a Government, we tried hard to shift accountability from measuring inputs to measuring outcomes. If we set schools an end goal such as the number of students studying the Ebacc subjects or having made progress throughout their time at school as measured by Progress 8, that should allow those working in our schools to use their experience to decide how to get to those end goals without the need for detailed instructions.

Another measure which I think will gain in importance as we have increasing amounts of data is the destination of our young people. What are they doing three, five and ten years after finishing full-time schooling?

If that approach is followed, and the evidence from employers is that character and non-cognitive skills help employability, then do we need to measure character? Is it not self-evident that those pupils who have the necessary traits and skills will score highly in the destination data?

If measurement is desired then would we measure each child's character or, rather, the school's efforts and programmes to develop character?

In addition, if the feedback from schools about the positive impact character education has on academic attainment is accepted then another way to judge whether a pupil has developed their character is not to measure it at all but to accept it as an innate part of their overall performance, which is measured via their academic attainment or other proxy measures.

When I asked the question about assessment at Gordano they pointed to their absence figures, where the school is below national average including persistent absence at 8.5% compared to a national average of 13.1%. At St James Primary School in the West Midlands they pointed to the fact that their reported incidents of bullying were down every year, reports about poor behaviour have gone down, problems and tense situations are calmed down more quickly and their attendance is up.

> *One of the important things about character education is surely that there isn't a 'right' way of doing it and that having a formal assessment process risks squashing the necessary innovation amongst schools and teachers.*

The risk with designing an assessment system for character is that it can drive perverse behaviour and lead to unintended consequences. One of the important things about character education is surely that there isn't a 'right' way of doing it and that having a formal assessment process risks squashing the necessary innovation amongst schools and teachers.

One of the great champions of character education, Sir Antony Seldon, has suggested having a "wellbeing or happiness measure"[14] – based on the fact that the Office of National Statistics produces a wellbeing or happiness index each year[15].

Former Cabinet Secretary Sir Gus O' Donnell has also advocated wellbeing league tables, in addition to academic league tables[16].

It seems to be helpful for each pupil to keep a record of activities which have helped them to develop character traits and demonstrate their personal values. This might apply equally to teachers as part of their CPD. And it is also important that a report on each pupil at the end of each term or year contains a section for a summary report on their character development to be given – demonstrating the school's commitment and each teacher's ability to assess and subjectively measure character and any changes.

One way of approaching this would be to follow the example of Therfield School in Surrey where each pupil has a 'Record of Personal Endeavour', known as ROPE. This allows students to record the activities they undertake which are deemed to give them the character traits the school wants them to develop. Each pupil's ROPE also provides a useful record for eventual university applications.

Having a record or journal allows students to reflect on what they have done and, just as importantly, what they have learnt. Self-reflection is a key character trait which needs to be developed. As Harrison, Morris and Ryan say in *Teaching Character in the Primary Classroom*, "The more that we provide children with a supportive environment where they can think back over recent events, examine what they were thinking and feeling and ask how they might act differently in the future, the greater the chance of them developing a sophisticated reflective capacity over time. It is this upon which virtue hinges."

14. www.buckingham.ac.uk/contact-us/information-for-the-media/press-releases/sir-anthony-seldon-calls-for-well-being-league-table-in-schools-on-a-par-with-exam-league-table/
15. www.ons.gov.uk/peoplepopulationandcommunity/wellbeing
16. Sir Gus O'Donnell interview, *The Times*, August 27, 2016

At King's Leadership Academy in Warrington, self-reflection is strongly encouraged using their ASPIRE model. Using examples such as mountaineers climbing Everest, the booklets which each student completes also ask them to make promises about their future work and behaviour. Students are required to be very honest with themselves about their current traits and attitudes and this covers not just their work but their personal approach to things such as getting to school, approach to lessons and learning and homework. They are also required to plan for future success, which reinforces the message that success doesn't just happen, it has to be worked at on a consistent basis.

Students are required to keep their self-reflection going and to reflect on how they see themselves at the end of the academic year. They are also introduced to fixed and growth mindsets. They are then expected to use all the points they have learned to plan their next academic year in the school.

It is a model that many adults could do with employing and is probably the sort of thing we often start on New Year's Day and abandon by January 3. At King's Leadership Academy, the need to be self-aware is constantly reinforced by the school's ethos and expectations for each pupil.

As Harrison, Ryan and Morris say, "At the heart of character education is enhancing pupils' ability to reflect critically on the situations and dilemmas they face. They need to learn to reflect upon and question their own actions and decide themselves what the 'right' thing is to do."

Cambridge Assessment has developed an online personal styles questionnaire, known as CPSQ, to help university admissions departments assess "behavioural styles which are important for higher education studies". It can be used to:

- help select students with the most potential to succeed
- identify students who are not a good fit with the course
- provide an early indicator of student development needs
- create a holistic view of student potential
- offer feedback to aid reflection and build self-awareness

The questionnaire results can be used alongside a candidate's personal statement, academic record and admission test results. No preparation is required to answer the questions and it is estimated that it will take up to half an hour for native English speakers to complete and up to an hour for those for whom English is not their first language.

CPSQ assesses five personal styles of behaving:

- Thinking style: Intellectual curiosity and open thinking
- Study style: Motivation to achieve and self-management
- Coping style: Resilience and adaptability to demands
- Interpersonal style: Social confidence and working with others
- Social style: Responsibility and risk taking

At the KIPP schools in the United States, character development is central to their whole approach. Progress is tracked through character growth teacher report cards.

Character Lab[17] has developed the Character Growth card which records the pupils own scores and also teacher scores. It is emphasised that the card should not be used to "diagnose or compare children, not to compare schools or programmes". The traits to be scored are curiosity, gratitude, grit, optimism, self-control (interpersonal), self-control (school work), social intelligence and zest. The grades run from recording that a student almost never demonstrates a trait to the student almost always demonstrating it.

An alternative is the Values in Action Youth Survey[18]. There is a version of the survey for 10- to 17-year-olds and a version for adults.

An alternative way is simply to include, as hundreds of schools have done for many decades, a summary in the school report written by a teacher or Head which focuses not on academic attainment but on each pupil's character and achievements.

---

17. characterlab.org/measures
18. www.viacharacter.org/www/Character-Strengths-Survey

If some form of measurement tool is needed then the next questions – what can be measured and how can it be measured? – have to be asked. It would be very possible to develop a tool such as Angela Duckworth's survey questions about a specific trait – such as, in her case, grit.

> *Simply asking the questions about character traits and development will focus minds on the importance of this and the priority given to it by a school and its leadership.*

Asking students to assess themselves or asking teachers to assess a pupil's character development – as with the school report example above – is possible. Simply asking the questions about character traits and development will focus minds on the importance of this and the priority given to it by a school and its leadership.

The Jubilee Centre for Character and Virtues has developed a character education self-evaluation handbook[19]. They recommend self-evaluation rather than self-inspection because the former offers more scope for bottom-up reflection and formative assessment. Of course, before embarking on any system of self-evaluation, the school must be clear exactly which virtues or traits they want students to develop.

The Jubilee Centre handbook states that there are three purposes for evaluating character education. The first is to see how a school's culture and ethos contributes to its character education. Secondly, to evaluate the effectiveness of a character education, strategy or approach, and third is to record self-reflection by students themselves. The handbook is

---

19. jubileecentre.ac.uk/userfiles/jubileecentre/pdf/character-education/EvaluationHandbook/
Section1_PlanningAnEvaluation.pdf

clear that "grades" for character must be avoided – the purpose of a self-evaluation exercise is more to form a character "picture".

The Jubilee Centre is clear that evaluating character is not easy and that "honesty and humility are called for due to the significant methodological limitations associated with evaluating character".

They suggest that the three components for evaluation are virtue knowledge, virtue reasoning and virtue practice. The first two, which can be grouped under the heading of virtue 'literacy', are probably easier to evaluate than virtue practice, which is described as "about using virtue knowledge and reasoning to promote virtue practice.

"Virtue practice enables people to give expression to virtue in desirable, recognisable and observable attitudes, behaviours and action. It involves translating virtue knowledge and reasoning into virtuous action and reflecting on how virtues were demonstrated and how strengths can continue to be developed and difficulties challenged. Observations on character would be the best method for evaluating virtue practice – but are difficult to conduct scientifically and ensure validity."

> *At King's Langley in Hertfordshire, lesson observations are carried out, but rather than assessing the knowledge content of the lessons, teachers can ask to be assessed on the way they are developing pupils' character through the lessons.*

Of course if character is being either specifically taught or included with the broader curriculum then the school leadership and outside agencies such as Ofsted could assess the teaching to ensure they do reflect the traits and values each school has identified as important. At King's Langley in Hertfordshire, lesson observations are carried out, but rather than assessing the knowledge content of the lessons, teachers can ask to be assessed on the way they are developing pupils' character through the lessons.

Emphasis has already been made of the need for a whole-school approach to character education and the adoption of key values which everyone from the Headteacher, all staff and all pupils work to demonstrate. So, another way of assessing progress is to assess the whole school and award some form of external recognition.

Gary Davis, the inspirational head of King's Langley in Hertfordshire, believes there is scope for some form of Government-backed character education kitemark which schools could work towards. The Values-based Education Trust set up by Dr Neil Hawkes already awards schools its own VBET award which involves external assessors from the Trust visiting schools and judging their work and achievements on values.

The Association of Character Educators is a voluntary membership organisation and has nine principles of character education which they state schools can use to audit, evaluate and plan their character education programmes against.

The Department for Education's Character Awards are a step towards a Government-backed kitemark – recognising award winners from each region of England and then having an overall winner allows schools to showcase not just their work to their peers but also to get national recognition for that work. Developing some form of kitemark based on the framework for evaluating award winners should be perfectly possible. Developing a specific measurement or assessment tool seems less desirable.

8

WHAT HAPPENS OUTSIDE SCHOOL

❝ WIDER CIRCLE

...it is also good for young people to meet others outside their usual circle of school friends, to belong to an organisation and to have additional opportunities to see adult role models and to develop good character in different settings.

❝ PARTICIPATION

But people have to want to participate and that is why developing that sense of community when a person is young, identifying a desire to 'belong' as such and then doing something about it is so important in developing character.

❝ NATIONAL CITIZEN SERVICE

Since the first pilots for 160 16-year-olds in 2009, more than 300,000 teenagers have taken part in NCS, making it the fastest growing youth movement of its kind for a century, and the largest programme for 16-year-olds in the country.

❝ BRIDGING THE GAP

Although many other organisations provide opportunities and activities outside school the literature on this topic suggests that schools are best-placed to provide extra-curricular activities.

❝ LEADERSHIP SKILLS

Another benefit of extra-curricular activities is the opportunity for participants to develop their own leadership skills. There will be more of an opportunity to work across different age groups and to practice skills such as coaching or organisation of younger participants.

I mentioned earlier the importance that schools such as King's Leadership Academy in Warrington attach to activities like the Duke of Edinburgh Awards and the research showing the positive benefits of being involved in the Scouts or Guides. As we have seen, character isn't just built in schools, and there are many extracurricular activities which happen outside education which develop the traits and values which young people need.

In this book I refer to extracurricular but many people use the phrase co-curricular instead in order to show these activities should be treated as equal to more academic curriculum studies.

In his 2016 Budget, the then Chancellor, George Osborne, allocated additional money to the Department for Education for a longer school day. Traditionally most state schools will finish between 3pm and 4pm and there may or may not be after-school clubs and activities which students then take part in. In the independent sector, the school day tends to be longer – until after 5pm – but more of the time is taken up by these extracurricular activities.

In *Our Kids*, Putnam says:

School-based extracurricular activities emerged roughly a century ago … the idea was to use extracurriculars to diffuse among all classes what we now call 'soft skills' – strong work habits, self-discipline, teamwork, leadership and a sense of civic engagement. But if we look at participation in extracurricular activities today – in everything from football to band to French club to the student newspaper – we can see yet another dimension of the growing class disparity in America's educational system.

He goes on to assert, "Noncognitive skills and habits such as grit, teamwork, leadership and sociability are unmistakably developed among participants in extracurricular activities." He points to 2006 research[20] which found that poor children are three times as likely as their non-poor classmates to participate in neither sports nor clubs (30% to 10%), and half as likely to participate in both sports and clubs (22% to 44%).

A further study found that during the past 15 years, activity levels in out-of-school clubs and organizations rose among affluent youth and fell among poor youth. From 1997 to 2012, the "extracurricular gap" between poor kids and non-poor children aged 6-11 nearly doubled, from 15% to 27%, while the comparable gap among kids aged 12-17 rose from 19% to 29%[21].

There will be many reasons behind these figures but family attitude, motivation, finances and the working patterns of parents amongst others must be key factors. As I mentioned in the Introduction, there is a reason why good parents ensure their children take part in extracurricular activities – although they can go overboard in ensuring every waking moment is full.

Sometimes it is good for a child's creativity and curiosity for them to be bored and have to find themselves something to do. But it is also good for young people to meet others outside their usual circle of school friends, to belong to an organisation and to have additional opportunities to see adult role models and to develop good character in different settings.

Of course, extracurricular activities don't have to be delivered by schools

20. Christina Theokas and Margot Bloch, 'Out of school time is critical for children: who participates in programs?' Research-to-Results Fact Sheet No. 2006-20 (Washington, DC: Child Trends, 2006)
21. Moore, Murphey, Bandy and Cooper, 'Participation in out-of-school time activities and programs' Child Trends Research Brief No. 2014-13 (Washington DC: Child Trends, 2014) – this includes both school-related and community-based activities

and teaching staff. However, almost every character award winning school facilitates the provision of such activities, perhaps by allowing premises to be used or encouraging staff to support such activities such as the Combined Cadet Force or, in the case of Therfield School in Leatherhead, Surrey, the teacher who set up and runs the school's climbing club.

Developing a sense of community is captured by the Jubilee Centre as 'Civic' virtues such as service and volunteering, neighbourliness, citizenship, community awareness and spirit and social justice. The intrinsic value is that such virtues help to promote the common good but they also contribute to personal flourishing by encouraging people to feel they are part of a group and have a wider purpose.

In *Of Good Character,* James Arthur says, "No explanation of character education can be complete without consideration of its sociological aspects. Character education, concerned as it is with ethical behaviour is pre-eminently social." Arthur believes that because Western society no longer has moral communities, "we are faced with the challenge of socialising children into good character in a situation that lays emphasis on personal autonomy and satisfaction."

> *In wanting to rewind the clock, many older voters are saying that they don't like the way society has developed and that the feeling of community spirit and cohesion has been lost.*

Arthur believes this needs a counterweight of emphasis on community – firstly the family and then wider society – and that schools play a crucial role in this process by "facilitating positive experiences of social interaction in an ordered context, and promoting mutual care and responsibility between its members". Schools play a role in bridging the gap between individual students and civic organisations.

Many commentators believe the language of individualism – the 'me culture' – is now so loud that the language of community is being drowned out. There are many who believe that this shift helps to explain the current rise in populist politicians and the desire for more Government intervention to address people's problems. In wanting to rewind the clock, many older voters are saying that they don't like the way society has developed and that the feeling of community spirit and cohesion has been lost.

This is undoubtedly true in many of our larger cities, but I would argue that outside many of our urban areas this is not true and that in fact there are many ways to increase people's sense of belonging – whether it is through sport, religion, politics and campaigning or through community activities such as community events to celebrate landmark occasions. But people have to want to participate and that is why developing that sense of community when a person is young, identifying a desire to belong, as such, and then doing something about it is so important in developing character.

One successful scheme which continues, rightly, to grow in national importance is National Citizen Service. Fifteen-to-seventeen-year-olds from all backgrounds come together as part of NCS for a shared experience lasting three to four weeks – mainly in the summer holidays, after GCSE exams. They push themselves out of their comfort zones in the great outdoors, learn important life skills (all whilst living away from home), and then work together to plan and deliver a social action project to make a difference in their community.

Since the first pilots for 160 16-year-olds in 2009, more than 300,000 teenagers have taken part in NCS, making it the fastest growing youth movement of its kind for a century, and the largest programme for 16-year-olds in the country.

NCS has proven impact, fostering trust and friendships across entrenched social divides; building skills for life and work, whilst widening horizons; and increasing levels of civic engagement and social action. NCS graduates are also equipped with the character strengths needed to flourish in later life, no matter what they choose to do. Their analysis shows significant and lasting impacts on levels of resilience, wellbeing and anxiety.

An IPOS Mori 2014 survey[22] of NCS participants showed that those who took part in the longer summer course believed the NCS had a positive impact on their personal resilience and cited things such as handling problems, getting over things going wrong, finishing things and learning from mistakes. There was a noticeable additional positive impact on those students eligible for free school meals.

The important thing about NCS now, and to give it the opportunity to be a truly one-nation scheme, is for every young person to take part in it. The cost of participating is already low and there is financial support available for those who are unable to meet even that cost. But NCS needs to become an automatic rite of passage for all British teenagers.

One of the other aspects examined earlier is how, if at all, the development of character traits can be measured and the traits themselves assessed. Schools across the country are showing this is, in many ways, possible and extracurricular activities are a part of this because the simple act of participation is, in itself, a demonstration of the acquisition of social capital and necessary character traits and values.

As the 2016 Social Mobility Commission Annual Report says, "The way in which children spend their time when not in school is not only important to their wellbeing and self-esteem, it can also contribute to their chances of accessing future opportunities." The Commission is particularly interested in examining the link between family income and access to participation in extracurricular activities.

---

22. www.ipsos-mori.com/researchpublications/publications/1784/National-Citizen-Service-2014-Evaluation.aspx

The Commission's report states that one study "found that 43 per cent of children whose mother had a postgraduate degree had music lessons, compared with 6 percent of children whose mother had no qualifications. At the age of 11, 85 per cent of children whose mother had an undergraduate degree participated in organised sport outside of school, compared with 56 per cent of children whose mother had no formal qualifications".

As I argue in Chapter 2, a government pursuing a true one-nation agenda cannot ignore such disparities in access to activities which we know shape a person's character. Activities outside the formal school day are important in encouraging a sense of achievement and also an increased belief that a person's own actions lead to positive change.

There are three broad forms of extracurricular activities – academic, non-academic and multi-strand extracurricular interventions. Academic means activities such as support with studies, non-academic includes sport and multi-strand could include extended schools. It seems that all types appear to have an effect on attitudes whilst academic extracurricular activities have the biggest effect on attainment – which is probably to be expected.

Although many other organisations provide opportunities and activities outside school the literature on this topic suggests that schools are best-placed to provide extracurricular activities. The provision by schools leads to positive associations by pupils with their school and its teachers. Clearly there is also the practical aspect such as the convenience of using a school site which is set up to keep students safe and the familiarity of the site.

There was a two-point increase in Key Stage 2 test scores for disadvantaged children who participated in after-school activities, which amounts to 40% of the inequality attainment gap.

Homework clubs lead to direct impacts on attainment. A study by the Nuffield Foundation published in 2016 showed that when measurement of the impact of extracurricular activities was specifically focused on disadvantaged children it was found that attendance at after-school clubs was the only organised activity that was significantly related to disadvantaged children's attainment at Key Stage 2. There was a two-point increase in Key Stage 2 test scores for disadvantaged children who participated in after-school activities, which amounts to 40% of the inequality attainment gap.

Other extracurricular activities shown to develop strong character traits include, of course, sport but also clubs and groups such as the Scouts and Guides. A recent study[23] showed there was a positive mental health effect associated with being a member of either group. The Scouts and Guides focus on an eight-point plan which focuses on character development as well as personal development, targeting attributes such as confidence, personality, motivation and charm and it is suggested the lifestyle of a Scout or Guide transitions into adulthood well.

In terms of schools prioritising extracurricular activities, it is known that at many schools there are weekly or even daily enrichment activities. At Ark schools, students who are behind in the curriculum are encouraged to take academic extracurricular activities and teaching staff are expected to run activities. Schools in the Ark chain are brought together for extracurricular activities. Similarly I was fortunate to attend the Harris Schools sports day at which the schools competed against each other.

A further example is the Duke of Edinburgh Award, and at King's Leadership Academy in Warrington every Year 9 pupil is enrolled in the Award as part of their character development programme. The 'Credimus' booklet provided by the school to its pupils states that a DofE Award is highly valued and recognised by colleges, employers and universities.

Achieving a DofE Award helps to bridge the gap between education

---

23. Jtech.bmj.com/content/early/2016/10/05/jech-2016-207898.full.pdf+html

and employment. King's Leadership firmly believe that, in taking part in a DofE Award scheme, their pupils will be investing in valuable skills closely link to their ASPIRE code. To achieve a Bronze or Silver DofE Award everyone has to complete all four sections – volunteering, physical, skills and expedition.

The booklet produced by King's Leadership to help its students achieve a DofE Award includes plenty of space for pupils to write up their own ascent to achieving an award. The booklet encourages self-reflection as well as planning activities and how to secure the necessary support to be successful.

Gordano school near Bristol attaches great importance to extracurricular options. The incredibly impressive and comprehensive list of options available forms part of the 'Gordano Guarantee'.

Options are grouped into seven types under the headings 'academic extension', 'activities', 'clubs', 'community', 'creative', 'events' and 'sporting'. Too numerous to mention here, they range from book club and creative writing to DofE to Lego club to Amnesty International to languages week and fencing. Interestingly, fencing seems to be a common theme because I watched a girls' fencing class on my visit to King's Langley. And out of 300 eligible students, 150 do DofE.

Gordano is explicit in setting out that extracurricular activities offer:

- New experiences
- Confidence and self-esteem
- Commitment to a goal
- Increasing depth and width of interests
- Positive attitude
- Learning time management and prioritizing
- Making a contribution
- Building solid relationship and people skills

As for the skills gained, the Gordano options booklet lists them as:

- Organisation
- Lateral thinking
- Practical
- Logical
- Analytical
- Interpersonal
- Persuasive
- Observational
- Communication
- Research
- Teamwork
- Creative

The options are provided thanks to the "enthusiasm and commitment of Gordano's staff".

Gary Lewis, the Head at Gordano, provided me with some analysis the school had done in 2015-16 about the gender breakdown of those involved in the clubs and also the involvement of pupils on pupil premium.

Fifty-four per cent of Years 7 to 11 girls were club members compared to 46% of boys in the same years. Forty-two children receiving pupil premium were doing one or more clubs, which was 24% of pupil premium students.

Gordano students are also involved in external organisations such as the Scouts and Guides and uniformed cadet services.

Every one of the secondary schools I visited offers some form of extracurricular or enrichment activities. The two are not necessarily the same although most will offer new experiences. Some, such as Therfield's rock climbing or Haywood's residential weekends, which involve staff and pupils, are directly relevant to building resilience in young people.

Another benefit of extracurricular activities is the opportunity for participants to develop their own leadership skills. There will be more of an opportunity to work across different age groups and to practise skills such as coaching or organisation of younger participants. Everyone gains from this. It can also be very positive for pupils to see their teachers in a non-academic environment where the relationship between teacher and pupil and therefore the role modelling can be seen in a different context.

There can be no doubt that extracurricular activities, in their broadest sense, offer the chance for those taking part in them to develop the skills and traits identified by Gordano. The concern is that not every pupil has either the opportunity or ability to pursue such activities. The most likely place they will get exposure to them – particularly schemes such as the Duke of Edinburgh Award, Young Enterprise, National Citizen Service and Youth Social Action – are not always available.

Many of these programmes have been working together since 2013 to amplify the value of social action through the #iwill campaign. Step Up To Serve, the charity co-ordinating the #iwill campaign, has monitored take-up of social action opportunities and how far schools and colleges have embedded them into their culture and practice. Their website provides useful resources for educators.

Even if school staff feel unable to offer such activities themselves, they should be strongly encouraged to facilitate their provision and to find out why some pupils are not taking part.

9

FRONTLINE FLOURISHING — WHAT SCHOOLS ARE ALREADY DOING

❝ SUIT THEIR COMMUNITIES

Each school mentioned here, and many others, have demonstrated their understanding of the importance of character education and their commitment to building pupils with great character and values. Each institution will approach this end goal differently and in a way to suit their communities.

❝ ENVIRONMENT

There seems little doubt that character can be effectively cultivated without explicit teaching. A child's environment is the key influence in developing character and should be the focus.

❝ HIDDEN CHARACTER CURRICULUM

Even those schools which might profess not to teach character will spend time building routines, implementing reward schemes and working on behaviour including skills such as self-control – in other words there is always a hidden character curriculum.

❝ COMMITTED

A school committed to development of character will identify the right method to embed different types of values and traits.

❝ TOOLS

The tools of great character education are available and there is an increasing understanding that without developing young people's values and therefore their character, the other parts of their education, and their future success in life, are less likely to hold good.

The intention of this book is to demonstrate not just why explicitly teaching character is both possible and necessary but also that it is already happening in many excellent state schools up and down the country.

Each school mentioned here, and many others, have demonstrated their understanding of the importance of character education and their commitment to building pupils with great character and values. Each institution will approach this end goal differently and in a way to suit their communities.

But there are some common themes which emerge – the need to identify the key values and traits; the need for school leaders to prioritise character development; the involvement of and role modelling by all staff as well as parents and the wider community; the investment by schools in the character and development of their staff; having some form of internal recognition of achievement as well as a way of encouraging self-reflection by students of their character development; the encouragement of extracurricular activities; and the fact that values and traits are evident everywhere and impact on every aspect of the school.

The greatest common attribute I found was that these are schools that say "yes" to opportunities which come their way – even if, at the same time, the Head is wondering how they will make the opportunity happen. As Sally Sixsmith, the Head at St James's Primary in the West Midlands, said to me, "We enter everything and take up opportunities offered."

How to get started? In his book *From My Heart: Transforming Lives Through Values*, Dr Neil Hawkes writes:

> If a school decides that it wants to implement the philosophy of valuing, along with its practices, then I would suggest that it invests in the following process that answers the question: How do you introduce values?
>
> The whole school community (staff, pupils, parents and community representatives) is involved in understanding, identifying and shaping the values education policy. A meeting or forum is set up to facilitate this process. The forum will propose that the school adopts universal, positive human values – such as respect, honesty and cooperation – to underpin everything it does (*ie* all administrative and organisational practices and the curriculum). These values are chosen through a careful process that involves thinking about what qualities (values) the school should encourage its pupils to develop.

Hawkes sets out the process he helped to run for one particular school involving a forum and debates which answered the question, "If you could encourage children to live one value, what would it be?" He also stresses that everyone must be involved in identifying the values the school is going to teach so that everyone feels ownership of the values. And, of course, the adults in the school will need to model the values – and Hawkes admits that often the most challenging part of the process is getting the adults to agree to do so.

The question asked of parents was, "Which are the six core values you would like us to instil in your child by the end of their time at our school?"

At St James's Primary School, the Head, Sally Sixsmith, and her Deputy, Lindsay Mason, explained to me how being a church school helped to instil their values. The previous Head had been in place for 25 years and Sally had been the deputy. When she took over Sally knew that there was much that was good about the school but also that it needed change.

Explicitly identifying the school's values seemed the right place to start. A sheet with a list of potential values was sent home with pupils so their parents could see what was proposed. The sheet was also shared with staff, governors and the pupils themselves. No one objected. It was made very clear that introducing values "should not just be another job for the staff". Sally and Lindsay are clear that by asking everyone it gave them ownership of the school. The question asked of parents was, "Which are the six core values you would like us to instil in your child by the end of their time at our school?" Eventually the following values were identified: respect, kindness, friendship, perseverance, honesty and responsibility.

A year later a questionnaire was again sent home asking parents if they had noticed how things had changed. The feedback from parents on the impact of being explicit about the school's values was very positive.

At St James's, the values are displayed everywhere and talked about all the time by the pupils – including by the wonderful group of very young children I bumped into as I left Sally's office at the end of my visit. They couldn't wait to tell me all about the values and how much they loved their school.

Staff meetings at St James's include discussions on values. In order to recognise achievements and effort, there is a house system and stickers are awarded. Pupils love telling Sally that they have another sticker. At the end of the week letters are sent home to the recipients telling families about the awarding of a sticker.

The school's values are part of induction evenings for new families, part of any tour of the school and part of the interview process for staff. Every member of staff role models the values and assemblies major on the value being discussed each half-term.

The story of King's Langley and its transformation from being in the bottom 3% of the country to being the second most improved has been told earlier in this book.

Gary Lewis, who became Head when the school was at its lowest, was clear that he wanted to see outstanding behaviour and outstanding morals. Every assembly has a relevant character theme and this is followed through into PSHE and registration and the virtues as identified by the Jubilee Centre are now embedded in the curriculum subjects too. Character language is on display throughout the school premises. CPD for teachers is a priority and each member of staff has eight half-hour 'pit-stops' each year to top up their thinking on the virtues.

Students are now being encouraged to apply for character leadership positions and in order to recognise achievements badges, headmaster commendations and credits are all part of the school's rewards scheme. The school also holds character discussions in their parents' evenings, which can produce some lively discussions.

At Tapton School in Sheffield the five "learning behaviours" which are tracked three times a year and awarded over nine levels are deemed essential within the school values and "not a bolt-on". They are discussed and referred to at assemblies (including particular 'aspiration assemblies'), in PSHE lessons, in staff training and with parents.

Executive Head David Dennis says that everyone "has to live this [approach]". Feedback to pupils has to be positive, critical and formative. The intention is to de-sensitise pupils to failure. Growth mindset evenings are held for parents of pupils in Years 7, 10 and 12. Extracurricular and super-curricular activities and volunteering opportunities are expected to be taken up.

Many schools focus, as part of their character education work, on the importance of learning behaviours. Traits such as resilience, resourcefulness, reflectiveness, reciprocity and respect, values and attitudes are used by Tapton School in Sheffield to judge each pupil's attitude and readiness to learn. There is also a strong commitment amongst staff towards their own continuing education through their Tapton Learning Communities. So, in this case it is the students' learning behaviour which is regularly assessed and reported on as well as what they are actually learning.

At Haywood Academy in Burslem near Stoke-on-Trent, Head Carl Ward talks about having to build the self-belief of his students when he arrived that they could get results. He introduced a new rewards system, based on progress, which recognises achievements every six weeks. Students get a score for everything they do and their achievements are reflected in a Commitment to Progress wallchart which is displayed in a prominent place in the school. Carl says that students now value the work they do in school.

> *Teaching staff are expected to contribute hours outside the classroom to work or activities with pupils but staff CPD is also highly valued.*

The school also wants to make the pupils feel special and for them to know their teachers really do care about them so there are residential weekends for the Year 10s and 11s run by the teachers. There are also after-school and holiday activities and the school library is open every day until 5pm. Teaching staff are expected to contribute hours outside the classroom to work or activities with pupils but staff CPD is also highly valued. The school has opened a sixth form and students are in academic, university-focused streams or work-based learning involving 1000 businesses offering work place opportunities.

Examples from King's Leadership Academy in Warrington are given elsewhere in this book. Character development is fundamental to the school's ethos and success. When the founders of the school first met they agreed they wanted to "re-vision education around moral purpose".

There is, deliberately, very much a can-do attitude about the school and everyone in it. From all pupils lining up in the playground twice a day, shaking hands with the teacher each time a class starts and entering the classroom, to each class reciting the school mantra at the start of lessons, the school's belief that "excellence is a habit" is on display. The school has a house system and a rewards system which gives each pupil a weekly statement on how many rewards they have collected and is intended to build delayed gratification.

Character and leadership skills are taught through various lessons – there is one hour a week led by the House tutor on the school's ASPIRE code which also weaves in PSHE topics. But character is not left to a stand-alone lesson. It permeates the whole week and is specifically referred to on every morning's briefing note. Years 7 and 8 study politics and public speaking and every seven weeks they have to make a speech. Leadership is also specifically taught for an hour.

The curriculum is arranged as five seven-week blocks and pupils undergo five assessments a year. By learning cycle seven they are expected to have picked up, accepted and dealt with any failures in their work.

The language of values is expected to be used in all lessons. Rather than saying that a student has been "naughty" they are instead told they "have not been professional". Values are talked about in assemblies and each form has to deliver assemblies. And values and the ASPIRE code are also raised at parents' evenings.

Staff training is very important. What is done for the pupils is mirrored for staff. Self-awareness and self-reflection is encouraged and all staff have a coach who they meet weekly.

At Babington College in Leicester, Principal Denise Newsome and Associate Headteacher Sara Fletcher talk about resilience being a key attribute needed by their very diverse intake and they also focus on

113

ensuring pupils are emotionally equipped for learning. This is "woven into the fabric" of the school and they have a Building Character for Learning (BCL) programme.

BCL objectives are set out on the board at the start of the lesson and referred to throughout the tuition. To reward achievements, BCL cards are awarded. The cards have to be handed over for the House Box. Every four weeks the cards are drawn out and rewards are given. The culture is positive so the pupils love getting the cards. Reports are given four or five times a year and the BCL awards recorded.

Extra challenges for the pupils can also be set – in the first week there were 800 extra challenges! Challenge cards are filled in and signed off and then go to the House prefects.

As in other schools, staff are very involved and there is a staff development group. Parents are also involved and on Wednesday afternoons there are activities for the whole school to be able to try something new.

Both the Gordano Guarantee and the Reflect tool have been discussed earlier in this book. Head Gary Lewis is particularly focused on developing 'stickability', self-esteem, the ability to reflect and resilience. The school has six Houses which are very important and pupils are very loyal to their House. Ofsted have commented that the House system is a strength and that it helps the Head of House to know parents and pupils as individuals. The school invites medal-winning sports stars and local business people into the school.

As set out in Chapter 8, Gordano prioritise extracurricular activities and all staff are expected to take on such activities – this can also be seen as an example of positive role modelling by staff.

Therfield School in Surrey demonstrates many of the attributes set out above. Head James Malley told me the school "always says yes". Character skills are discussed in tutor time and the school also has a House system and a myriad of badges are awarded to reward pupils. Some of the pupils I met had barely any space left on their lapels which was great to see. The school focuses on excellence and leadership and opportunity. A different character trait is prioritised each half-term. Senior students mentor other students. In particular, team building for the Year 7s is carried out by the sixth formers, which benefits all of them.

Elizabeth Garrett Anderson has a diverse intake in North London. The school aims to build confidence in all pupils and having an academically rigorous curriculum is part of that. There is also an emphasis on growth mindset and reflective learning. The school's ethos is that there should be no limits on any pupil's ambitions and abilities but also that "EGA girls are kind".

In Years 7-9 there is a bespoke skills programme taught across a double period each fortnight. The Assistant Head is specifically charged with developing wider links outside the school, overseeing extracurricular activities and a longer school day. The school finishes early on Thursdays so there is time for extracurricular activities, including Duke of Edinburgh, and CPD for staff. Coaching for staff and students is available. Female role models are very important. There are specific themes for the Years 7-9. Year 7s are studying how to be outstanding learners, Year 8s how to be outstanding citizens and Year 9s focus on work-related learning and their futures.

What the above examples show is that these schools have a whole-school approach. They educate for character both explicitly and implicitly. Teaching about values, virtues and character traits and the way in which they are developed happens in dedicated time in the curriculum but those values, virtues and traits are also embedded in existing school systems and curricula.

Is there a correct balance between explicit and implicit character education?

Explicit character education requires students to reflect on aspects of their character and this is likely to be reinforced by explicit teaching on character and values in time set aside for that (including assemblies) as well as bringing out moral or ethical discussions in other subjects.

Implicit character education includes embedding character and virtues in school structures and the curriculum and creating a school culture which recognises and rewards certain behaviours and demonstrations of character skills, virtues or values. Character is also demonstrated implicitly by teachers and other staff modelling good character and strong virtues or values.

Although extracurricular activities are important in the development of character and underlying values and such activities require specific time to be set aside, the link is not always spelled out as clearly as it is at Gordano, so such activities probably fall under the implicit heading.

To break it down further, character education, as well as being explicit or implicit, can also be embedded in the school or discrete. So explicit but embedded teaching would include discussions on values as part of the existing curriculum. Explicit but discrete teaching would include time set aside for lessons ethics or teaching of growth mindset or meta-cognitive strategies as well as time for students to complete their records such as Gordano's Reflect tool or Therfield's ROPE. It would also include the curriculum at King's Leadership which includes examination of leadership within the usual subject curriculum but there is also, for both students and staff, specific leadership programmes of study. Students studying at the highest level and staff alike follow courses of study set by the Chartered Management Institute.

Implicit character education is embedded via teaching the curriculum without highlighting the character points, a behaviour reward system which offers no commentary and teacher modelling or pedagogy which is not commentated on. Implicit but discrete character education includes activities which happen outside the classroom and might even happen outside the school.

At the heart of all of this is the question: does character need to be explicitly taught or can it be left to being caught? There seems little doubt that character can be effectively cultivated without explicit teaching. A child's environment is the key influence in developing character and should be the focus. However, it cannot be ignored that a child's school is a major part of their environment as they grow up and learn about the world around them. So that is why at school the influencing is likely to involve explicit efforts to shape behaviour and form good habits.

Even those schools which might profess not to teach character will spend time building routines, implementing reward schemes and working on behaviour including skills such as self-control – in other words, there is always a hidden character curriculum.

> *"If we acknowledge our duty to teach character, we should similarly acknowledge our duty to do so consciously and deliberately."*

And, if those routines, reward schemes and focus on particular skills and behaviours are likely to have a powerful effect on a student in addition to the taught curriculum, as Harrison, Morris and Ryan argue, a school has a duty to reflect critically on that hidden curriculum and its impact so that it is no longer hidden.

They argue that, "to say 'we do this anyway' is to acquiesce to a second-best state of affairs which abdicates us as educational professionals from our responsibility to refine and improve our practice. If we acknowledge our duty to teach character, we should similarly acknowledge our duty to do so consciously and deliberately."

Harrison, Morris and Ryan state that there is a difference between learning about virtue and learning to be virtuous. Knowledge alone cannot guide actions. This requires deliberate teaching rather than just relying on the school ethos to somehow seep into a student's mind and guide their future behaviour.

Given the lack of robust evidence and the pressure on curriculum time, most schools are wary of devoting specific curriculum time to explicit character lessons. To what extent and how character is malleable is still largely unknown. The EEF research mentioned earlier may help to demonstrate the extent of any malleability and which interventions work best.

The evidence collected by schools such as the University of Birmingham School will be very valuable, although, as discussed elsewhere in this book, assessing character development is not an easy thing to do. Instead, many commentators assert, character will follow from a school focusing on its key priorities properly. As Robert Peal, the author of *Progressively Worse*, writes:

It is sometimes observed that here independent schools lead the field[.] … [This is due] to a clear articulation of the schools' values[.] … The furniture of school life means that positive character traits are a lived reality not a one-hour-a-week timetabled subject[.] … I would say that the biggest barrier to effective 'character building' remains poor discipline. Clear rules and structures form our pupils' habits, and their habits come to constitute their character. This has been central to virtue ethics since Aristotle, who argued that 'we enter the palace of reason through the courtyard of habit'.

As Gary Lewis, Head at King's Langley, found, good character starts with good behaviour – behaviour here being used in its widest sense. Schools therefore need to focus on embedding character through behaviour systems and the school ethos, supported by an explicit commitment to character traits (to capture the assertion by Sally Sixsmith at St James's that "values are displayed everywhere") and a rigorous curriculum.

This triangle means:

- Habits of good character are fostered through the school's behaviour system, approach to learning and a consistently maintained ethos. For example, traits such as self-reliance, perseverance and confidence are promoted through teachers' messaging on learning and expectations and respect and politeness are taught through modelling and through holding students to account for poor behaviour;

- A rigorous curriculum supports intellectual and performance virtues and allows students to more meaningfully explore moral problems;
- And in order for good habits to be chosen and internalised rather than simply enforced, schools must make explicit the value of good habits and encourage reflection. For example, calling out dishonesty over a piece of work; or explaining that a request to re-do a piece of work is made to build a student's ability to improve; or assemblies which reinforce school-wide values and encourage reflection.

A school committed to development of character will identify the right method to embed different types of values and traits. If we go back to the original Jubilee Centre list of four virtues – performance, intellectual, moral and civic – then some will best be required to become habits through an overall school ethos of high expectations that performance virtues will be demonstrated in lessons and that moral virtues will be demonstrated in behaviour throughout the entire school day. The school's commitment to these values is likely to be shown through explicit praise when the virtues are demonstrated by students.

A rigorous curriculum develops intellectual virtues (curiosity, resourcefulness, good reasoning) which can be praised when demonstrated in the classroom and therefore requires curriculum content which demands mastery from all pupils and sets high expectations for all pupils. King's Leadership produce an impressive booklet entitled Pedagogical Practice for teaching staff which covers the school's philosophy – "Glass ceilings are not acceptable" and "Outstanding teaching is prerequisite for student success" – as well as how to put their philosophy into practice in planning, in the classroom and how to be consistent in everything that a member of staff does.

Character education is flourishing on the frontline of many of our schools. Some have prioritised it and made it much more explicit than others. The tools of great character education are available and there is an increasing understanding that without developing young people's values (and therefore their character), the other parts of their education, and their future success in life, are less likely to hold good.

How do we make the leap then to getting every school and teacher to put character education into practice?

10

WHAT NEXT?

GOOD EDUCATION

Good character education is good education and vice versa. It is in society's wider interest for all young people to develop good character and virtues. Schools have a clear role in helping this to happen.

GROWN ORGANICALLY

Legislation or guidance from the Department for Education is definitely not the answer. The growth of character education and giving everyone working with young people the confidence to talk about values needs to be grown organically.

PARENTS AND GOVERNORS

Building parental demand and demand from governors for a values-driven school and a focus on character development is important too.

RESPONSIBILITY

Taking responsibility for our situations and our behaviour whether as students or adults is liberating. Being able to reflect on ourselves – whether it is about a piece of work or our own conduct is tough but rewarding.

DESERVE

Every child deserves to gain both great knowledge and character from their time in education. Everyone working in education deserves to work in environments with a clear values-driven ethos.

Good character education is good education and vice versa. It is in society's wider interest for all young people to develop good character and virtues. Schools have a clear role in helping this to happen.

I argued in the Introduction that change in education doesn't happen by accident. It needs a deliberate push. Public awareness needs to be raised, government needs to make it clear to those in the education system that this is a priority and they will support it and, most importantly, the frontline – namely schools, Heads, teachers, governors and communities – need to be enabled to create the conditions to allow systemic change to happen, to take hold and to grow.

Legislation or guidance from the Department for Education is definitely not the answer. The growth of character education and giving everyone working with young people the confidence to talk about values needs to be grown organically. It is best delivered by enthusiastic advocates to groups of Heads and teachers, as I saw Steve Harris from Wellbeing Education do in Leicester one snowy January Friday morning.

Government can of course provide incentives and recognition – which is what we did with the Character Awards started in 2015. A number of schools I visited told me that they didn't really consider what they were doing to be 'character education' until they saw the specification for the awards and realised they fitted the criteria.

Awards given by other third party organisations such as the Association of Character Educators, IPEN and the Values Based Education Network are invaluable in spreading the word amongst schools.

> *In fact, all adults could probably do with thinking about the values we model to those around us. That's why the parents' evenings at which values are discussed are so important but can be tricky.*

The best advocates are of course the students themselves who demonstrate in their daily lives the values and traits they have learnt and those staff who also benefit from modelling the values their school focuses on. In fact, all adults could probably do with thinking about the values we model to those around us. That's why the parents' evenings at which values are discussed are so important but can be tricky.

Building parental demand and demand from governors for a values-driven school and a focus on character development is important too. If this book can prompt a wider discussion about the values on display in our education system, the traits that our education system is currently developing and how we all have the power to ask the schools we are involved with what their values are and what their approach to character education is, then so much the better.

For a school embarking on explicit character education for the first time the identification of the values and development of the curriculum will be time consuming and require extra resources and effort. But the resulting more-focused school will be worth the work needed to get there.

In my experience, the greatest frustration in life comes from feeling that someone else has control of that life. Taking responsibility for our situations and our behaviour whether as students or adults is liberating.

Being able to reflect on ourselves – whether it is about a piece of work or our own conduct – is tough but rewarding. Knowing that at a moment of maximum tension or pressure we have the tools to make the right decisions, even if no one else is looking, builds our confidence in ourselves and respect from those around us.

Character education provides the framework for all those elements. It shouldn't only be open to some pupils at some schools. Every child deserves to gain both great knowledge and character from their time in education. Everyone working in education deserves to work in environments with a clear values-driven ethos. This is possible but it can't be left to someone to think about on a wet Wednesday when everything else has been done.

Character matters. It has mattered at all points in history, but in today's increasingly complex, challenging and fast-moving world I believe it matters more than ever. The English education system used to do character development very well.

So, we can rediscover that imperative and get this right for the next generation or we can get it wrong and fail to unlock their true potential. Character in the 21st century needs to be taught and not just left to being caught by chance.

What's your next step?

Appendix

In order to be able to advise Ministers accurately and impartially, civil servants often commission research and reports. This research is in addition to any research or trials conducted by bodies such as the Education Endowment Foundation, as mentioned in this book.

Ministers won't necessarily see such research in full but it does help officials to answer questions such as *What's the current thinking on this?*, *How do we show this is the right and necessary step to take?* and *What do we do next?* Such research is all about making good and evidence-led policy decisions.

Government-commissioned research is made publicly available in accordance with a Government Social Research protocol. This allows such research to be shared and, if appropriate, challenged. It also helps to improve the transparency of policy-making.

What is interesting about the research that follows here, published in August 2017, is how widespread the desire is to develop many of the traits mentioned in the book, and how few schools actually think of this as 'character education'.

There is also a strong focus on mental health running through the research, demonstrating the link between the two areas. There are some clear conclusions and recommendations and it is to be hoped these will be used by the Department for Education in developing the next stage of the push towards deliberate character education in England's schools.

Nicky Morgan

Department
for Education

Developing character skills in schools

Summary report

August 2017

Natcen Social Research & the National Children's Bureau
Research and Policy Team

Social Science in Government

Contents

The research

This report provides a summary of the key findings from the Department for Education (DfE) research into the provision of character education in schools. The DfE commissioned this research to understand how schools in England currently develop desirable character traits among their pupils, and to explore their experiences of this. The production of robust national estimates and a qualitative understanding of provision provides the evidence base for future policy and research.

The research included a national survey of provision and case studies exploring decision- making, models of delivery and experiences of different approaches to developing character, followed by a workshop to consolidate learning from the research.

This report summarises part of a wider, mixed methods project exploring mental health and character education provision in schools and colleges across England.

Policy context

There has been growing interest in character education over the last decade. There has been increasing recognition of the role that certain character traits or attributes such as resilience, self-regulation, and emotional and social skills can play in enabling children and young people to achieve positive health, education, employment and other outcomes[1][2][3].

The DfE understands character education to include any activities that aim to develop desirable character traits or attributes in children and

---

1. Morrison Gutman, L. and Schoon, I. (2013) *The Impact of non-cognitive skills on outcomes for young people* London: EEF and IoE.
2. Durlak, J., Weissberg, R., Dymnicki, A., Taylor, R. and Schellinger, K. (2011) "The Impact of Enhancing Students' Social and Emotional Learning: A Meta-Analysis of School-Based Universal Interventions" *Child Development* 82(1): 405-432.
3. Arthur, J. and O'Shaugnessy, J. (2014) Character and Attainment: Does Character Education make the grade? Birmingham: Jubilee Centre for Character and Virtues.

young people. The DfE believe that such desirable character traits:

- Can support improved academic attainment;
- Are valued by employers; and
- Can enable children to make a positive contribution to British society.

Accordingly, since 2014, the Department has announced a number of investments into character education, including funding for provision and research into effective practice.

Research aims

A significant, multidisciplinary field of theory and research is emerging around how best to conceptualise character education[4], identify what works in influencing children's character development[5,6], and explore the relationship between these traits or attributes and academic and other life outcomes[1,2,7]. The DfE commissioned this research to understand how schools in England currently develop desirable character traits among their pupils, and to explore their experiences of this. They intend for this evidence to provide a basis for future policy and research.

The aims of the project were to provide

1. Robust national estimates on the activities and support provided by schools to support character education;

2. Qualitative evidence to explore different approaches to and experiences of developing character traits; and

4. Jubilee Centre (2017, revised) *A Framework for Character Education in Schools* Birmingham: University of Birmingham.

5. Berkowitz, M. and Bier,M. (2006) *What Works in Character Education: A Research driven Guide for Educators.* Washington, DC: Character Education Partnership.

6. Early Intervention Foundation and Education Endowment Foundation (2015) Introductory presentation at EEF and EIF Resilience, *Character and Social and Emotional Skills – where next for Education Policy* event, London, 22 October.

7. Arthur, J., Kristjansson, K., Walker, D., Sanderse, W. and Jones, C. (2014) *Character Education in UK Schools* Birmingham: University of Birmingham.

3. Examples of specific activities that schools have found to be effective.

Methodology

The research formed part of a mixed methods project investigating mental health and character education provision in schools and colleges in England through a quantitative survey and qualitative case studies.

The survey of character education provision was conducted in the final term of the academic year, 2015-16 (8th June to 1st August 2016). The primary aim of the survey was to gain a representative profile of provision within schools and other educational institutions, as well as providing an understanding of the issues that institutions face in delivering character education. This is the first time that a robust nationally representative survey based on a stratified random sample of schools has been carried out to assess the provision of character education[8]. Overall, 880 schools completed the character education survey[9] (see Table 1 below). The majority of participants were senior leaders: head teachers or other members of the senior leadership team, meaning that the findings generally reflect the viewpoints of these staff. It was beyond the scope of the survey reflect the judgements of a range of other staff members within the same institutions.

---

8. More detail on the quantitative sampling approach is provided in the full report – Marshall, L; Rooney, K; Dunatchik, A; and Smith, N. (2017) *Developing character skills in schools: Qualitative case studies*

9. Though weighting can eliminate some element of non-response bias, it is important to recognise that schools with more active programmes may have been more inclined to agree to participate.

Table 1 Total achieved sample[10]

Institution type	Population	Issued	Achieved	Response Rate
Primary local authority	13,561	2,640	316	12.0%
Primary academy	3,056	667	94	14.1%
Secondary local authority	1,071	970	87	9.0%
Secondary academy	2,076	667	95	14.2%
Independent schoo	1,861	666	64	9.5%
Special school	1,545	666	137	20.6%
Alternative provision & pupil referral unit	339	291	87	29.9%
Overall Total	**23,855**	**6,567**	**880**	**13.4%**

In order to extend learning from the survey,[11] case studies were conducted in a cross section of mainstream schools, special schools and pupil referral units (PRUs) between September and December 2016. The case study sample was drawn from the sample of schools that had completed the survey, and was purposively selected to focus on mainstream primary and secondary schools that were more actively engaged in provision aimed at developing pupils' character traits. Two special schools and two PRUs were included in the sample to provide transferable learning about more specialist practice11.

The case studies were followed by a workshop held at the DfE in January 2017. Participants from case study sites were invited to take part in the workshop to consolidate learning and further develop practice recommendations and conclusions from the research.

---

10. Independent schools, special schools and alternative provision/PRUs are not reported by phase as the majority of these institutions operate on a combined basis across both primary and secondary phases.
11. More detail on the qualitative sampling approach is provided in the full report – White, C; Gibb, J; Lea, J; and Street, C. (2017) *Developing character skills in schools: Qualitative case studies.*

Key findings
How do schools understand their role in character education?

Almost all (97%) schools sought to promote desirable character traits among their students, although fewer (54%) were familiar with the term 'character education' prior to being approached to take part in the research.

In line with this, case study participants did not naturally use the term 'character education'. However, when prompted, they equated the term with support for pupils' (personal) development as well-rounded individuals[12]. The development of character was seen to be embedded in the school and integral to its overarching aims and purpose, rather than a stand-alone set of lessons or activities. Case study settings viewed their role as being to:

- Encourage pupils to understand, value and demonstrate the positive behaviour traits that would make them well-rounded, grounded citizens;
- Support the development of the skills required to function in and contribute to society;
- Support social and emotional development, in order for pupils to better understand themselves and work on their weaknesses; and
- Instil pupils with a moral compass and skills in understanding and interacting with other people.

What motivates schools to seek to develop positive character traits?
Schools primarily aimed to develop character in order to promote good citizenship (97%) and academic attainment (84%). Across all school types, the character traits most highly prioritised were honesty, integrity and respect for others (a high priority for 94% of schools). Less importance was placed on curiosity, problem-solving and motivation,

---

12. During the case study research participants were asked about developing character traits and attributes but these were not terms or concepts respondents used. Therefore, the term "developing character" was used to describe the holistic approach undertaken by schools and colleges.

although these traits were still a high priority for more than two-thirds (68%) of schools.

Beyond these key objectives, the aims of character education varied across different types of institutions. For instance, secondary schools were more likely than primary schools to link character education to employability (86% vs. 46%). In addition, special schools and alternative provision (including PRUs) were less likely to focus on improved academic attainment, and were more likely to report supporting the development of certain character traits for reasons other than improving academic performance, employability or citizenship.

Priorities also differed according to:

- **The needs of pupils.** Case study PRUs and special schools particularly emphasised the importance of resilience, self-esteem and self-regulation in enabling their pupils to overcome barriers to learning. Schools in deprived areas underlined their responsibility to nurture positivity and self-belief around achievement and combat low aspirations.
- **The religious values of the school.** Faith schools drew upon their heritage and identity to identify particular traits of importance, and to assert the centrality of character development to their purpose as a school.
- **Relevant policy, research, theory and practice.** School approaches had also been influenced and driven by previous government agendas (e.g. British values[13]); and theory, in particular values-based education, the Growth Mindset approach and strengths-based approaches.

What activities and approaches do schools use to develop positive character traits?

Most schools used school-wide, cross-curricular approaches to develop character. Almost all (97%) had a mission statement or set of core values intended to contribute to character education, and assemblies (92%) and

---

13. DfE (2014) 'Promoting fundamental British values as part of SMSC in schools: Departmental advice for maintained schools'.

subject lessons (89%) were both used to develop desirable character traits among pupils by the vast majority of schools. A significant minority (41%) of schools offered distinct character education lessons. In addition, almost all (97%) schools used extracurricular activities to develop character traits. Sports and/or performance arts clubs (91%), outward bound activities (72%), hobby clubs

(71%) and subject learning clubs (60%) were each used to develop character by a majority of schools. In the state sector, secondary schools were on average more likely than primary schools to use extracurricular activities as a means of developing desirable character traits. In particular, secondary schools were significantly more likely to use subject learning clubs (87% vs. 57%), role model sessions (80% vs. 39%) and volunteering or social action opportunities (76% vs. 35%) to develop desirable character traits among pupils.

The qualitative research found that, in case study settings with high level of provision, key messages and values were promoted and reiterated at different levels in order to embed character education across the life of the school. Assemblies, tutor time, PSHE[14] lessons, SMSC[15] and extracurricular activities were all cited as opportunities to '*drip feed*' the desired messages to students and encourage them to reflect upon, develop and demonstrate character traits. Staff-student relationships were also seen as key, with staff modelling desired traits and being approachable and engaging to encourage students to be open with them and take on board their advice.

What institutional processes are in place to support character education?
Just fewer than one in six (17%) schools had a formalised plan or policy in place for character education. Nevertheless, the qualitative follow-up found that schools without formalised policies were able to point to other documents that evidenced their approaches to developing certain character traits.

---

14. Personal, Social, Health and Economic
15. Spiritual, Moral, Social and Cultural Development

A quarter (25%) of schools had a dedicated lead for character education. The case study research found that it was typically head or deputy head teachers or other senior leadership team members that headed up schools' approaches to developing particular character traits, often recruiting a small team with relevant skills to support them in developing and delivering the provision across the school.

In addition to these dedicated staff, heads emphasised the importance of encouraging all staff to take responsibility for developing pupils' character traits or attributes. While these schools were selected because of their high level of commitment to character education, the survey found that a significant minority (43%) of schools offered all staff members training relating to the development of character traits among pupils.

Analysis of survey findings found that the significant minority of schools undertaking highly visible, planned, reflective and specific approaches to character education (including dedicated staffing and explicit character education plans and policies) were most likely to make use of a range of activities to develop character traits and attributes.

What challenges do schools face?

The biggest barriers for schools seeking to provide character education centred around competing demands on staff time and capacity. The qualitative research found that the school-wide nature of character education made staff capacity particularly important for successful delivery. Staff time was not only needed to deliver specific provision, but also to ensure that key aims and messages were embedded across the curriculum, and understood and committed to by all staff. Competing time pressures were reported to largely come from the introduction of new curriculum specifications and pressures such as performance-related pay and inspection requirements that encouraged schools to focus on academic subjects and results. Allocating staff time to deliver character education, sharing ideas and resources amongst staff, and having a culture where staff felt valued themselves and could understand the benefit of character education were identified as essential in overcoming this staff capacity as a barrier.

Although other challenges and barriers such as a lack of engagement from pupils or parents and a lack of knowledge or information were reported in the survey, these were only experienced by the minority of schools. The case study research uncovered other challenges and barriers to provision, notably a lack of funding for extracurricular provision and difficulties in measuring pupils' character development and thus demonstrating the value of provision.

What do schools think is key to success?

Successful character education was felt to depend on a **clear vision and whole school approach embedded across the curriculum**. It needed to be driven forward by **strong leadership**, and delivered and modelled by staff with the appropriate skills, time and access to activities that could be tailored appropriately to the needs of students.

School staff felt that recognition needs to be given to the importance of developing character in pupils. **Resources and skills** are required to support practice in developing character, alongside other requirements for academic success. Teachers needed to be **encouraged, developed and supported** with activities to develop character traits in their pupils.

In addition, participants felt that the **government and wider sector** could helpfully support schools by:

- Investing in teachers' time and capacity to focus on developing pupils' character traits and attributes
- Creating a database of organisations providing guidance, resources and tools for developing character, and a network for schools to discuss and share practice
- Developing a menu or bank of tools and activities that have been proven to work 9
- Providing tips on how to monitor pupils' character development and the impact of provision

Conclusions

This research aimed to investigate what schools in England currently do to develop character traits and attributes among their pupils, and their experiences of putting this provision into place.

Overall, the study found a strong commitment to character education in schools across England. Schools highlighted the pivotal role they play in providing character education and understood it to be integral to schools' overarching aims and purpose.

The development of desirable character traits was seen to enable children and young people to become well rounded individuals capable of reaching their potential both personally and academically. However, the specific aims of character education differed according to the needs and circumstances of pupils.

Almost all schools sought to promote the development of desirable character traits. Most schools used a range of school-wide, day-to-day activities to develop these traits or attributes, including curricular and extracurricular provision.

Few schools reported a lack of priority for character education. However, a lack of time and capacity was identified as a key constraint. Key facilitators were a shared vision and strong leadership for character education. Schools reporting highly visible, planned, reflective and specific approaches for character education were more likely to offer a range of provision.

Though this research identified some factors that schools felt were key to success, it did not attempt to capture the quality or effectiveness of current provision. The DfE intend for this work to provide a foundation for further investigation, including research into effective practice and gaps in provision.

Department
for Education

Report authors: Lydia Marshall, Clarissa White, Robert Wishart, Allison Dunatchik, Jen Gibb, Jo Lea, Cathy Street and Neil Smith

© NatCen 2017

Reference: DFE- RR697a

This document is available for download at www.gov.uk/government/publications